D0345384

Norman Vincent Peale

Ruth Stafford Peale

Discovering
The Power
Of
Positive Thinking

By Norman Vincent Peale

The Amazing Results of Positive Thinking
Enthusiasm Makes the Difference
A Guide To Confident Living
Have a Great Day—Every Day
How To Be Your Best
In God We Trust
Inspiring Messages for Daily Living
The New Art of Living
Norman Vincent Peale's Treasury of Joy and
    Enthusiasm
Positive Imaging
The Positive Power of Jesus Christ
The Positive Principle Today
The Power of Positive Living
The Power of Positive Thinking
Power of the Plus Factor
Sin, Sex, and Self-Control
Stay Alive All Your Life
The Tough-Minded Optimist
The True Joy of Positive Living
This Incredible Century
You Can If You Think You Can

By Norman Vincent Peale and Smiley Blanton

The Art of Real Happiness
Faith Is the Answer

By Norman Vincent Peale With Donald T. Kauffman

Bible Power for Successful Living

By Ruth Stafford Peale

Secrets of Staying in Love

Discovering
The Power
Of
Positive Thinking

by
Norman Vincent Peale
Ruth Stafford Peale

PEALE CENTER
FOR CHRISTIAN LIVING
The Outreach Division of Guideposts
66 East Main Street, Pawling, N.Y. 12564-1409

SPECIAL PEALE CENTER EDITION

Published by Peale Center for Christian Living
66 East Main Street
Pawling, NY 12564-1409

CONTENTS

INTRODUCTION

My father, a minister of the Gospel, believed in God, but he didn't always believe in himself. Norman Vincent Peale was a shy, tentative boy, yet, as he matured into manhood, his faith led him to the conviction that God had placed a portion of His power in all of us. My father reasoned, if this was the case, then each of us was capable of doing great things. This line of thinking changed him from a tongue-tied introvert into a genial minister who wholeheartedly embraced the Bible as an infallible guide for creative living. His upbeat, positive approach began to electrify his congregations.

When my father met and married Mother, Ruth Stafford, his expansive geniality was given a new force by her practical spirituality. And so it is with the book you now hold in your hands. Part I was originally written by my father as a series of lessons on positive thinking. He intended them as basic guidelines for reaping the benefits of positive living. Part II, written by my mother, Ruth Stafford Peale, explores practical, specific methods for dealing with life's everyday challenges.

The overall message of *Discovering the Power of Positive Thinking* is simply this: If you believe that the power of God within you is equal to any of life's difficulties, then a rewarding life will be yours. This belief inspired the best-seller, *The Power of Positive Thinking*, and sustained my mother and father's love for life, for one another and for the millions who continue to embrace their ministry. It has worked in my life, and it can work in yours, too.

—*Elizabeth Peale Allen*

Part I:

Norman Vincent Peale

CHAPTER 1

How To Become A Positive Thinker

This is the day the Lord has made; I will rejoice and be glad in it. —*Psalm 118:24*

L ET'S LOOK at the question: How do you start being a positive thinker? The start is like all beginnings: first a child, then an adult; first kindergarten, then ultimately the university; first a duffer, then an accomplished golfer. So the person who deeply desires to be rid of negative thought habits and become a positive thinker must humble himself to the status of a beginner, as a music student starts with finger exercises.

1. Speak in Positives. The first step is a simple one: stop speaking in negatives or in an indifferent, lukewarm way. Instead, begin to speak in positives. How we speak has a profound determination on how we think.

Spoken words tend to drive deeply into your consciousness to emerge finally in thought patterns. Your ear hears what your lips say. Accordingly, a message is immediately flashed to the conscious mind, and if a statement is repeated often enough, it is sent on to the deep unconscious. Then your conscious mind begins to obey the images sent to it by the unconscious, which has been conditioned by your speech habits.

It is most important at the start, and indeed always, to carefully watch every word you utter, however seemingly commonplace. The elimination of habitually used negative words and statements will not come easily, but it is not impossible to achieve. Remember—*it is not impossible.*

The writer Napoleon Hill wanted to write books. But he was a poverty-stricken, uneducated boy and was told that his dream was impossible, because, in order to write he would need to understand and know how to use words. Painstakingly, he saved his money and bought a dictionary so he could study words. His first act was to cut the word "impossible" from the dictionary. He then threw it directly into the wastebasket. But, more importantly, he cut the word "impossible" from his mind. You will need to do the same.

Tomorrow morning, instead of saying, "It's going to rain and be a bad day," say, "We are going to have a wonderful rain today. There is no such thing as a bad day. It's going to be a good day."

Memorize the following affirmation. Repeat it three times every day: "This is the day that the Lord has made; I will rejoice and be glad in it" (Psalm 118:24 KJV).

2. Choose To Be Happy. As you awaken, say aloud: "I have two choices for this day; to be happy or to be unhappy and I choose to be happy." Your startled ear, hearing you speak these strong words, will flash that assertion to your astonished consciousness, which will then oblige you by making it a happy day for you. Remember this important fact, that the mind will ultimately obey all your commands when spoken firmly and authoritatively.

3. Affirm the Good. Look for every opportunity during the day to speak the good word; to say something hopeful and optimistic to everyone you contact. Insert a positive into all conversations. If, for example, someone negatively asserts that the country is going into a decline, do not argue, but express your faith in the future. As you go about affirming the good, not only will you bless other people, but you will develop yourself as a positive thinker.

To sum up, we end where we began with the important speech principle—never talk negatively or in a half-hearted way, for in so doing you tend to develop negativism in your thoughts. Speak always in positive terms about everything, about everyone, about yourself. By the process of positive speaking you will, in time, become a positive thinker.

You don't have to be great to start, but you have to start to be great. —Joe Sabah

CHAPTER 2

How To Keep Positive Thinking Going

I have come that they may have life, and that they may have it more abundantly.

—John 10:10

READERS of my books on positive thinking have sometimes asked the question, "How can I keep positive thinking going when the motivation that gave rise to it tends to decline?" The students point out that through the reading of my books, they became inspired and motivated and everything went so much better for them. But with some hard knocks and setbacks along the way, the going began to get tough.

As a result, inspiration started to fade and motivation declined. Negative thinking began taking over again. So then, in desperation, they wrote to ask how to keep positive thinking going always—how to restore vitality to it in those down periods, which seemed to come at times. And, of course, this is an important question for those who want to qualify as positive thinkers and live successfully.

1. Keep Your Level of Positive Thinking High. It must be recognized that there is a variation of mood, a sequential up and down in human emotional periods. And this rhythmic rise and fall of motivation must always be considered in the effort to maintain the positive at higher levels.

Get in your mind, and firmly hold, the vital understanding that positive thinking brings up and sustains at higher levels the motivational attitude, even with the above mentioned variation, than the level would have been had you continued as a negative thinker. With positive thinking, the high level mark goes higher and the low level mark never sinks as low, so that even though the rise and fall of moods is a fact of human nature, the total rise and fall and rise again comes out at an upper level. The higher, therefore, that you keep the range of your positive attitudes, the less will be the fall-off even during a down period. Thus you will learn to keep the ups always up.

2. Give Thanks. Take 15 minutes every morning regularly for an inventory period. Make a mental list—to write it down is still better—of every good thing in your life. Add them up and you will say, "Why this is simply terrific! How greatly God is blessing me."

Use this affirmation, "God is good. God is surrounding me with opportunity. He is filling my life with blessings. He is pouring happiness into me. Praise the Lord. Thank you, Heavenly Father." Turn to John 10:1-10 in the New King James New Testament and commit to memory these words, *"I have come that they may have life, and that they may have it more abundantly."*

3. Renew Your Attitude. To keep positive thinking going strong, regular renewal of attitude is required. You will encounter negative viewpoints constantly and therefore your own positive attitude will continually be subject to possible erosion. To counteract the influence of such negative thoughts, read positive books and periodicals. Associate with positive-minded people, attend positive thinking rallies. In short, keep your thought processes within the positive climate as far as possible.

Find a church where the pastor teaches a positive life view, where the capacity to believe is stressed and the power of faith is taught and practiced. Become part of such positive fellowship. In so doing, you will find strength to continue in a positive way and you will also be supported by other like-minded people.

I know of a man who became a church member, but whose pastor not only did not practice positive thinking, but went further and attacked the positive concept in his sermons. This man, believing in his pastor's guidance, became a confirmed negative thinker and continued so for nearly twenty years. During this time he experienced many reverses, so much so, that, he says, "Everything was coming unglued."

He then started reading *The Power of Positive Thinking* and other books in which a positive mental attitude is taught. He began to acquire a new concept of the Bible as the greatest of all books of faith. Result: His life took on new meaning. He recovered from a potential failure situation and through new thought processes became a successful and happy man.

He said, "I prayed myself out of the negative into the positive and when, now and then, I begin to slip back, I know what to do. I just pray myself back into the positive."

Search the Scriptures for powerful verses of faith; mark them and make them yours. The Bible is full of them. When down moments come, fall back on these verses. Say them aloud and walk forth boldly on the great promises of God who created you in His own image—strong and positive.

I discovered I always have choices and sometimes it's only a choice of attitudes.

—Judith Knowlton

CHAPTER 3

Train Your Mind

I can do all things through Christ who strengthens me.
—Philippians 4:13

B Y THE PRACTICE of positive speaking, that is, by firmly telling your mind that you mean to develop a positive attitude, you may be sure that your mind will accept your new determination. It may accept it grudgingly and perhaps doubtfully, for, since you have been negative (or at least non-positive) for so long a time, your mind naturally may be excused for being dubious about your positive intentions.

But having made the determination and spoken positively, insisting vocally that you are now committed to the positive way, your mind can do no other than to acquiesce with your determination. The mind knows who is the real director of your personality, and though, in the past, you may have believed that thoughts control you, it is actually true that *you* control your thoughts.

1. Take Charge of Your Thoughts. So, therefore, the first principle in training your mind to think positive thoughts is to begin taking your rightful place in your personality and assume a sovereign control over your mind and what it produces. Take charge of your thoughts, for you can do what you will with them. Affirm the authority of the believer as stated in Luke 9:1, "Then he called his twelve disciples together and gave them power and authority over all demons, and to cure diseases."

Also affirm William Ernest Henley's great line in "Invictus": "I am the master of my fate, I am the captain of my soul." Practice seeing or visualizing yourself as the director of your thoughts, the authoritative supervisor of your mind.

But you must be prepared for resistance on the part of your mind. It will not easily let go of the control it has exercised over you during your negative thinking years. It will vigorously protest this new positive treatment, but if you persist and tighten your control over your thoughts, your mind will finally surrender and obey your commands.

One of the mind's clever little tricks, in its attempt to reassert and hold on to its authority, is to suggest that your new positive attitude won't really work. That it is only a passing phase and that you aren't really the positive type anyway. When this happens, as no doubt it may, just remember that wise old saying, "You cannot prevent the birds from flying over your head, but you can keep them from building nests in your hair."

You cannot prevent such thoughts from coming, but you can keep yourself from holding them in mind. Every time you repudiate such a defeatist thought, it will grow weaker and ultimately will leave you alone as the conqueror of your mind, the sovereign controller of your thoughts.

2. Fill Your Mind With God. A sure method of training your mind to think positive thoughts is to "fill your mind full of God." The phrase was first used by Howard Christie, famous American artist, who was an expert positive thinker. When I asked his secret he answered, "Every morning I spend fifteen minutes filling my mind full of God. Then no negative thought can possibly enter my mind for it is repelled by the God thought."

William Manchester in his book *American Caesar,* the life of General Douglas MacArthur, tells that in every military crisis of the General's eventful career, MacArthur always first retired to read the Bible. He thus fortified himself against all negatives in the situation and kept his faith strong, which may explain much about his many victories.

3. Look Positively at Every Problem. Systematically, look at every difficult problem. Then deliberately take a positive attitude toward each one by asserting, "To every disadvantage, there is a corresponding advantage." Keep looking positively for that advantage. Say that affirmation aloud so that your consciousness may continue to pick up your vocally expressed determination. This will stimulate your progress in a marked and definite manner.

Drive deeply into your thought process the greatest of all faith thoughts, such as the following: "I can do all things through Christ who strengthens me" (Philippians 4:13) and "If God is for us [for me] who [or what] can be against us" (Romans 8:31). Underline these verses in your Bible and commit them to memory. They will nurture the positive attitude.

It isn't what you know but what you are willing to learn. —Cliff Schimmels

CHAPTER 4

Who Says Positive Thinking Is No Good?

Bless those who persecute you; bless and do not curse.

—Romans 12:14

I WAS ASKED what to do when someone tells you that positive thinking is "no good." Let us consider that question. As you go forward in the adventure of learning to be a positive thinker, you are likely to meet some persons who will depreciate positive thinking as a "Pollyanna" exercise, or as a get-rich-quick scheme, or as a visionary procedure that is superficial and without value.

I know that this will happen to you, for it certainly has happened to me. I was roundly condemned by a small, but vocal minority. But today many of those who were part of that negative chorus are now loud in praise, and indeed are themselves practitioners, of positive thinking.

In fact, the concept of positive thinking gained general respect as one of the most vital and viable creative living techniques of our time. So do not allow the condemnatory attitude of one who is hostile deter you from your right to hold a contrary viewpoint and be a positive thinker.

Just because someone tells you that positive thinking is no good does not make it so. That is merely his or her opinion, and since the critic has not studied or worked with positive thinking, that opinion is hardly authoritative or entitled to respect as a valid judgment.

1. Analyze Positive Thinking. Any adverse opinion is entitled to consideration. And this one gives us a chance to analyze positive thinking, evaluate what it has done for us and form our own opinion, whether it is "no good" or, on the contrary, "very good." And if, after careful and honest evaluation, you find that positive thinking is a good thing and of value, then, of course, you are entitled to ignore the "no good" label and proceed to forget it as of no importance. Always, when you have rationally given consideration to an emotionally-motivated criticism and found it lacking in substance, the part of wisdom is naturally to let it concern you no more.

2. React to Criticism Scientifically. The positive thinker actually becomes expert in handling criticism, not only of positive thinking, but in whatever area it is leveled against him or her. The positive thinker takes what we call a dispassionate attitude—one without heated emotional reaction. In fact, he approaches the critic scientifically, asking, "Is this criticism based on an honest difference of opinion, devoid of any emotional motivation, or is it tinctured with dislike or resentment or some other non-intellectual factors?" He asks reflectively, "What dictates the hostile and adverse attitude of this person?"

As a result, one is better able to meet the criticism and indeed to be helpful to the critic.

3. Help Your Critic. The positive thinker will, of course, want to take a positive and creative attitude toward the critic so that he or she may enjoy the same benefits that we have found in positive thinking. It may be that the critic tried positive thinking and the effort was not made effectively. Therefore, poor results were encountered, all of which turned him off. Perhaps the effective positive thinker might actively endeavor to help the disillusioned person to find the great values that he has found. Read Romans 12:9-21 and pay extra attention to verse 14: "Bless those who persecute you; bless and do not curse."

I recall a woman who wrote me a critical letter voicing the opinion that positive thinking had no value and condemning me in strong terms for foisting these "stupid and worthless ideas on the public." Her lack of restraint and the personal character of her criticism led me to conjecture whether she was emotionally upset or had experienced some failure of her faith in a crisis.

I called her long distance and quietly thanked her for her letter and expressed interest in helping her. She became quite reasonable and tractable and explained that she had an alcoholic husband. She had come to believe that by "sending out positive thoughts" to her husband she could cure him of alcoholism. It seemed he had come home in an especially bad condition, beat her and smashed the furniture. In her grief and anger, she decided positive thinking was no good and she resented me for writing a book on the subject.

We discussed how best to deal with her husband. I suggested she hold a mental image of him as a well man, that she put him in God's hands and, more importantly, that she give God plenty of time with him. At my suggestion, when I got to know him, the husband joined Alcoholics Anonymous. He wanted to change and got to believing that he could with the Lord's help. He has been "dry" now for several years.

The wife continues to hold the image and the image has developed into fact. She told me, a bit contritely, "You are nice for not getting mad at me." I replied that in my own way I'm a teacher and a teacher should never react emotionally to his students. In fact, I did not blame her for her exasperation. Anyway, she has become a competent positive thinker, and she is an enthusiastic believer that positive thinking is very, very good.

Actually, we must realize that many people have been raised as negative thinkers. When a baby is born, he or she is by nature positive. Everything is great. But as the child grows up, it may be in a home where a negative thinking climate prevails. Accordingly, he becomes negative in his attitudes. Such thinking becomes habitual. When finally he meets positive thinkers, they seem to have perhaps an extra cheery attitude and this irritates him—perhaps challenges him—as it did this woman in the story above. So he resists change, and change often comes hard.

In the process of change, this habitually negative thinker fights the new concept, calling it "no good," "a phony idea" and other uncomplimentary terms. But even so, he wants to be free of the old restrictive ideas that are holding him back.

Our job is to understand and help him through a new truth process that can be painful. So the idea is, love the critic, be patient, understand and help. That is the way of the positive thinker, who takes a positive attitude toward everyone, even his critics.

The best way to destroy your enemy is to make him your friend.   —*Abraham Lincoln*

CHAPTER 5

What To Do When Things Look Bad

Be strong and of a good courage; be not afraid . . . for the Lord thy God is with thee whithersoever thou goest. —Joshua 1:9

HOW DO WE THINK positively when things look bad? It must be understood that positive thinking is not a fair-weather philosophy nor is it designed for those times when things are going great. Positive thinking is a tough formula for tough times. It is really at its best when the going gets hard. As the well-known slogan of a famous football coach has it, "When the going gets tough let the tough get going." That is where and when positive thinking really comes through.

So when things look bad, here are a few suggestions for bringing positive thinking creatively into the situation:

1. Look for the Advantage. Realize the great truth that to every disadvantage there may be, and usually is, a corresponding advantage. Consider the old truism that behind the darkest clouds, the sun is shining. In the toughest situations, there is always some value that is inherently good. But if you should not find such value after a persistent search for it, the positive thinker, by looking for the good, for the advantage, for the sunshine, will do better with the difficulty. Far better than the negative thinker who sees only the bad. What you deeply think has a strong tendency to produce itself in fact. So always think positively, believingly, expectantly, hopefully.

Perform the above consistently and you may have the experience of the man I met one snowy morning in St. Louis. When the wakeup call came in my hotel room the telephone operator said, "It's a bad day—deep snow." The taxi driver who took me to the railroad station, since no airplanes were flying, darkly observed that it was "a bad morning." So did the porter who helped me with my bags. By common consent, it was a "bad morning." Wind was blowing snow from the train-shed roof onto passengers.

Then I saw an obviously happy man coming along, his face wreathed in smiles. "Hello, Dr. Peale," he exclaimed, "Isn't this a glorious bad morning!"

I was so fascinated by this expression that on the train I asked him how he had developed his positive attitude. "I used to see the dark side of everything until I found Jesus Christ. Then I started walking on the sunny side of life," he explained. "So when things go badly, or seem to, that is the time to think and affirm God's good."

2. Turn Impossibles into Certainties. The important emphasis when things are not going well isn't what is happening but your attitude toward what is happening. A friend once gave me a wall plaque that reads: "Attitudes are more important than facts." At first, I doubted the truth of that statement, but it proved itself so many times that I owe much to it as an insight.

Let's assume a big, hard fact, and there are two men of equal intelligence facing it. One man says, "This is a very harsh fact, a big, overwhelming difficulty. This is more than I can handle." So he is defeated by the fact.

The other man says, "This is indeed a tough fact, a very big, difficult proposition, but even so, with God's help I can handle it." And he proceeds to do it successfully. It is the attitude toward the fact that is crucial and determinative more so than the fact itself.

Let me tell you of two elderly positive-thinking ladies, friends of mine. One lives in Paris, the other in Toronto. The Paris lady had deep trouble but surmounted it. Asked how, she replied, "I learned to put thoughts of God up against my trouble."

The Toronto lady had a leg amputated at age 84 but did her housework from a wheelchair. Her 28-year-old granddaughter came twice a week "to be cheered up by Grandma." When asked if she ever became discouraged, her answer was, "Certainly I do."

"And what do you do when discouraged?"

"Do?" she replied. "What is there to do but get over it? I simply take the attitude that, with the Lord helping me, I can sweep all dark shadows from my mind, as I do the dust in my house." These two women have become experts in positive thinking. They repudiate the dark view.

3. Look Up Not Down. I have often had to deal with glum and discouraged people who have said, "I've hit bottom and there is no hope." To one such man I replied, "Congratulations. Having hit bottom, you can go no lower; the only direction is up. So start thinking up." He did and, after a time, new ideas came that helped him to move up well above the bottom.

"Now," he said, "I'm actually glad to know that bottom is down there to shield me from further decline in the future." He had actually turned the bottom into an asset!

I met a man who said, "My mind is like an elevator. I press a positive thought button and move up to a higher floor."

William James said, "Our belief at the beginning of a doubtful undertaking is the one thing that ensures the successful outcome of your venture."

Also, commit to memory this powerful statement from Joshua 1:9. "Be strong and of a good courage; be not afraid . . . for the Lord thy God is with thee whithersoever thou goest."

Be not afraid. Believe that life is worth living, and your belief will help create the fact. —William James

CHAPTER 6

Visualize!

For where two or three are gathered together in my name, there I am in the midst of them. —Matthew 18:20

I WANT TO SHARE with you a very important lesson on a vital principle of thought and attitude. It is called visualization. It may also be termed the imaging or picturization principle.

There is a deep tendency in human nature to become precisely what you habitually imagine or "image" yourself as being. Image yourself as a defeated and inferior person and all the forces of your personality will conspire to make you just that. For example, if you picture yourself as sick and weak, and if you hold that image long enough, you will strongly tend to become sick and weak.

On the other hand, if you picture yourself as healthy and strong with lots of vigor and energy, and persistently hold in your mind that self image, your entire being, body, mind, and spirit, will work together to make you that kind of person.

The late William H. Danforth, founder of the Ralston Purina Company, a large corporation, was my inspiring friend. As a boy, he was skinny, weak, and sickly. But he had a teacher who taught him to "see" himself as strong, robust, and vigorous. "I dare you to be the strongest boy in the class and you will outlive all your classmates," said his teacher. Ultimately, he did. When Mr. Danforth was well into his 80s, he demonstrated his exercise program, which itself required extraordinary energy. He wrote a book called *I Dare You,* which I regard as one of the greatest motivational books. In it, he dares the reader to image, to visualize, and become whatever he wants to be that is good and right.

1. Hold Your Image. Hold the image of what you want to be physically, mentally, and spiritually, and what you want to be in business, in love, in life itself. Hold that picture or image tenaciously in your conscious mind until, by a process of intellectual osmosis, it sinks into the unconscious mind. And when it does, you will have it because it will have had you—all of you.

2. Be Specific. There is an amazing power in the strongly held and directed image to effect desirable change in yourself and in your life. To accomplish such change and improvement, the image must be specific and exact even as to detail and timing. The realizable wish, a strong factor in psychology, will respond as desired to the degree to which the desire is specified, then held without deviation and believed in completely.

Have a goal, not a fuzzy goal, but one that is sharply defined. Hold it in consciousness until presently the subconscious takes it over. As Dr. Smiley Blanton, the eminent psychiatrist, said, "God presides in the subconscious." That is where the power of personality lies, and it has incredible strength to produce what the convinced person wills.

Then pray about your imaged goal to be sure it is a right objective, for if it is not right, it is wrong, and nothing that is wrong ever turns out right.

3. Visualize Your Wish as Happening. Know what you really want: Visualize it not as something you hope or vaguely wish to happen, but something you believe is now happening, now actually being, in essence. For spiritual help, read, "If two of you agree on earth concerning anything that they ask, it will be done for them by my Father who is in heaven" (Matthew 18:19). Also Matthew 18:20: "For where two or three are gathered together in my name, there I am in the midst of them." These verses describe the principle of the two or three. I can assure you on the basis of personal experience there is power in it. How does this work?

One night I spoke about positive thinking in a city auditorium and was challenged later by a lady in a rather strange manner. She demanded that I guess her age, which I thought to be 50 but didn't commit myself. Actually, she was 35 and had an obesity problem. "Can positive thinking make me thin and how can I reduce?" she asked, telling me she was five feet in height and weighed 190 pounds.

"What do you want to weigh?" I asked. "Oh, I don't know. I just want to get thin."

"How thin?" I persisted. "You must have a precise goal." After discussion, we settled on 120 pounds as a desirable objective. "Now, when do you want to achieve this weight."

"Oh, I don't know. As soon as possible, I guess."

I insisted upon a specific date and we selected a date eleven months hence. I then drew a human form and asked what she wanted her bust, waist, and hip measurements to be. I wrote alongside the picture the figures she gave.

I handed her the drawing, suggesting she have it copied and carry one copy in her handbag, paste another on her mirror and stick one on the refrigerator door—especially the refrigerator!

"Oh, I just haven't the strength to diet. I've tried it so many times," she said despondently.

"But this time it's going to be different, for you have the creative image principle going for you. Every day you will 'see' yourself becoming thinner and trimmer." And then I told her about the two or three principle I have mentioned and offered to join her in a spiritual agreement that, with God's help, she would gain this victory. She stuck to it, getting a big kick out of her ability "to say no to sweets," as she put it, and she achieved the imaged weight by the specified date.

The visualizing or imaging procedure of the positive thinker in achieving desired results has been personally demonstrated by many persons. I am reminded of the rather aimless young man who said he wanted to "get somewhere."

"Where?" I asked. "Oh, I don't know," he replied. Further questioning revealed that he did not know when he wanted to get there, or what he wanted to do.

"We have got to tighten up your thinking," I told him. I asked him to go home and read Romans 8:31-39 and to underscore verse 31: "What then shall we say to these things? If God is for us, who can be against us?"

I knew it could "buck up" this young man's faith in God and in himself as a child of God. I told him to write his goal, with the date to achieve it, on a card and place copies where he could see them constantly. He was to give me a copy, too, so we could work together on the two or three principle. He reached his goal by the specified date and since then has achieved other goals by the very same method!

As you work toward becoming a real positive thinker, use the visualization principle, picture yourself accomplishing it, and you will achieve it.

Change starts when some-one sees the next step.

—William Drayton

CHAPTER 7

Apply Positive Thinking to Any Situation

If thou canst believe, all things are possible to him that believeth. —Mark 9:23

NOW LET'S CONSIDER: Can you apply positive thinking to any situation? The reasonable objective should be to make something better out of what is, or what it seems to be. Even if a given situation is apparently filled with all manner of foreboding and unpropitious factors, it is always possible, by the creative insights of positive thinking, to turn up potentials and possibilities that negativists would never discover.

A man who influenced me greatly in my youth, who built a very prosperous business against great odds, used to say, "Even the worst problem has a soft spot." He would actually simulate "walking around" a problem, poking at it with his crooked arthritic forefinger. I watched with fascination as, with a positive attitude, he would inevitably find a way to overcome many situations that baffled other less positive people. Naturally, such a man attained positive results out of all kinds of seemingly unpropitious situations.

1. Develop a Sound Philosophy. Sometimes, problems seem so difficult, and are so many in number, that one tends to become frustrated and perhaps even overwhelmed by them.

I met a man on the street one day who actually told me he would give a substantial sum of money to my church if I would get him rid of all his problems. Disclaiming any power to do that, I asked if he meant that he wanted to be rid of his most difficult problems, or perhaps most of his problems. "Certainly," I said, "you do not mean that you want to be free of all your problems."

"The latter is what I want," he responded gloomily. "I have had it." "Well," I told him, "in that case, I think that possibly I can help you," and stated that I had recently been in a place "on professional business" where the head man said there were 100,000 people and not a one had a problem.

The first enthusiasm I had seen in this man manifested itself. "Lead me to that place,' he demanded.

"I don't think you will like it," I said. "It's a big cemetery."

2. See Problems As a Sign of Life. It is a fact that no one in a cemetery has a problem, for they are dead. It follows, then, in logical sequence, that problems constitute a sign of life. Perhaps, the more problems one has the more alive he is.

Few of us really like problems but, since they are an inherent part of life, they must have a purpose. And it could be that the Creator had in mind the development of strong people. A person can hardly become strong without being subjected to difficulty, adversity, hardship. That is the way individuals grow strong. Cultivate this positive concept of a problem in your development as a positive thinker and your creativity will be greatly enhanced.

3. Give it Your "All." Positive thinking may be applied effectively and creatively to any situation if you give the situation your whole mind, your entire thought, your full purpose, your sincere faith in God. Don't be a hold-out. Be *an all-out*. Positive thinking is an all-out mental state. And in it the spiritual is a powerful force.

One student of positive thinking qualified quite well except that he was unconsciously a "holdout," only partially committed to a goal. He would attend my speeches given in various places and would say, "I have half a mind to give this or that project a go." At first, this phrase went unnoticed. Then it protruded in so many conversations with him that I concluded it represented a basic attitude —a half-mindedness. When I faced him with this conclusion and pointed out that his efforts to have the full benefit of positive thinking were being, in fact, frustrated by his half-a-minder attitude, seeing this fault clearly, he at once began to develop as a whole-minded person. The result was successful performance of high order.

In *The Power of Positive Thinking*, I wrote about a man who was at the height of his power.

"You amaze me," I commented. "A few years ago you were failing at everything. Now you have worked up an original idea into a fine business. You are a leader in your community. Please explain this remarkable change in you."

"Really it was quite simple," he replied. "I merely learned the magic of believing. I discovered that if you expect the worst you will get the worst, and if you expect the best you will get the best. It all happened through actually practicing a verse from the Bible."

"And what is that verse?"

" 'If you canst believe, all things are possible to him that believeth' (Mark 9:23). I was brought up in a religious home," he explained, "and heard that verse many times, but it never had any effect upon me. One day, in your church, I heard you emphasize those words. I followed your suggestion of putting myself in God's hands and practiced your outlined techniques of faith. Along with that, I try to live right. "I guess it's a kind of miracle, isn't it?" he asked as he concluded his fascinating story.

Change your mental habits to belief instead of disbelief. In so doing, you bring everything into the realm of possibility.

Our prayers are answered not when we are given what we ask, but when we are challenged to be what we can be. —Morris Adler

CHAPTER 8

Are You a Positive Thinker? Test Yourself

But one thing I do, forgetting those things which are behind and reaching forward to those things which are ahead. —*Philippians 3:13*

O DEVELOP as a positive thinker, it is helpful at intervals to appraise your progress by measuring how well you are doing. Are you really moving away from negativism? Are you truly beginning to activate positive responses and attitudes in your life? Are you making a definite break with the tendency to look at things from a pessimistic point of view? Have you arrived at the place in your thinking where it is becoming instinctive for you to think positively, rather than being forced to repel negative thoughts first before a positive attitude takes over?

Well, then, how can you test whether you are, in fact, becoming a positive thinker? Here are some ways:

1. Evaluate Your Desire To Be Positive. Ask yourself how deep-seated your desire is to become a positive thinker. You have had the impulse to become positive in your thinking. Does that impulse, which may be, as the word implies, "impulsive," have tough, continuing power? If the desire has deepened and grown stronger and urgent to such an extent that it simply will not be denied, then you can indeed say, "Yes, I want with all my heart to become, and constantly be, a positive-thinking person." You are on the way—a long way—toward your objective!

A young man wanted a job, but the job market was sparse. He was told he couldn't get a job "for love or money." But he argued that a deep desire is always matched by a compensatory satisfaction of such desire. So he knew that he could bring the desire and the satisfaction together, which he proceeded to do.

Only deep desire can attract a goal. Therefore, if the desire to be positive in nature is operating at full strength in your mind, you are definitely moving toward becoming a positive thinker.

Ask yourself these questions: "Has the number of times I now make a negative remark lessened?" And: "Does my daily conversation contain more positive affirmations than formerly?"

Our speech does indeed betray us. What we really think is bound to slip out. Instinctively, we tend to form in words the kind of thoughts that are germinating in our mind. So make a careful check list of the things you say in a given day. If negative statements are markedly declining and positive statements are noticeably increasing, you may take it for a fact that you are moving in the direction of becoming a real positive-thinking individual.

2. Keep Optimism Going. Another test of your positive thinking is your attitude toward adversity or setbacks. Do they throw you or are you now able to shrug them off and keep optimism going? To what extent do adverse circumstances depress your spirit?

If you find yourself with a dogged attitude of "so what, I can take that," then you can know that positive thinking has really taken firm hold in your mind. And when, finally, you come to the mature level where you can actually see and appreciate the value of adversity, you will have moved to a high place on the positive scale.

The late J. C. Penney was a great friend of mine. Once I asked him the secret of his outstanding success in life. Without a moment's hesitation, he replied, "Adversity and Jesus Christ." And he continued, "Without both, I would never have amounted to anything." Mr. Penney believed that adversity develops spiritual and mental muscle for the positive thinker. And, of course, Jesus Christ gives the strength to stand up to it and the wisdom to weave it into your life pattern to make you strong

What is the current status of discouragement with you? Do you tend to become discouraged less of the time, but still are troubled because you, now and then, are discouraged?

We must realize that rhythm is in all nature, in the rise and fall of tides, the coming and going of seasons.

Rhythm is also in the human nature and is evidenced by moods, sometimes higher and, at other times, lower. But as long as this variation moves up and down from a reasonable level, it is normal. All that is required is to just hang in there on the downsweep of the pendulum and ride up on the upward sweep. If you are developing the ability to handle your down moments and compensate them upwards, you are mastering thought control, which is, of course, one of the marks of a positive thinker.

3. Keep Faith in Yourself Strong. To sustain a powerful, undeviating faith in your future is the attitude that marks one as a positive thinker. Belief that goals can and will be attained, that you will find a significant place in life, that you will be a truly successful person—that is the secret of creative living. *Believe in God, believe in life, believe in yourself and in your future.* Think future, pray future, believe future. How do you check out on that test?

I once knew a man who wanted to become a positive thinker and he did so magnificently. But he was not doing well in the business he was in. However, he was able to handle discouragement. He went to a wise counselor who analyzed his abilities and suggested that he was cut out for the restaurant business. He and his wife teamed up. She had a flair for menus and decor, he for food management. Together they built a small chain of the finest restaurants—a highly successful enterprise. His strong faith in himself was verified.

In the New Testament locate, read, and then commit to memory the following from Philippians 3:13: "But one thing I do, forgetting those things which are behind and reaching forward to those things which are ahead."

So keep that belief and faith in yourself going always. The extent to which you are doing that right now is an indication of your progress as a positive thinker.

Doubt makes the mountain which faith can move.

—Decision

Part II:
Ruth Stafford Peale

CHAPTER 1

Combating Loneliness

Behold, I am with you always, even to the end of the age. —Matthew 28:20

" I AM SO TIRED of being lonely and going places by myself." This sentiment is echoed by many people. Loneliness is a problem that affects each of us at some time. Not many of us can get through life without feeling it. I read a report from a UCLA social psychologist stating that ten percent of the American population feels lonely at any given time. Because most people are afraid to admit they feel lonely, you have to assume that this number may be much higher.

I've had personal experience with this feeling. Ever since Norman passed on, I've felt a tremendous void in my life. And although I'm blessed with a loving and supportive family, some of whom live close by, I am still painfully aware that my lifelong companion is not physically by my side. Losing my best earthly friend hurts, but I cannot let this feeling consume me. There are important things left for me to do while I'm still here, projects that will make Norman smile up in Heaven.

For the past few months, I've been successfully combating my loneliness. You can, too, by doing the following:

1. Go Out of Your Way for Someone. When we're alone, many of us tend to spend time dwelling on our loneliness, on our problems, on past mistakes. This is unhealthy. It feeds upon itself until the spark of one's personality is devoured. The best antidote I know of for people caught in this trap is for the lonesome one to go out of his or her way for someone else.

The gestures you make toward other people need not be elaborate. The important factor is to make loving contact with others. The simple process of thinking of nice things to do for others is enough to get your mind off your own problems. And this is one of the first things you must do to pull yourself out of this discouraging state of mind.

For example, send a distant loved one a note, expressing your feelings toward him or her. Or give a neighbor with an infant the coupons you receive for baby products. You can also go out of your way for strangers by doing simple things such as letting the elderly person in line behind you at the grocery store go ahead of you. Complimenting a store employee on good service is another simple way of showing care. If you look around, you'll discover many ways to extend yourself to others. And, you'll find that the more you do for others, the more you do for yourself. You'll like yourself better, and so will others.

I recently read an amazing article about a man who has extended his entire life for one other person. Not many of us can do what he has done, but, as you'll see, the experience has been as fulfilling for him as it has for the person he's helped.

Jim Newman, an 80-year-old Texan, first met Michael Harris in 1984. Michael, who is profoundly mentally handicapped and suffers from cerebral palsy, lived in a nursing home that the widowed Newman frequently visited.

Soon after their meeting, the then six-year-old boy and the elderly gentleman became fast friends. Newman saw the boy nearly every day. He was there to help with Michael's hygiene, to give the boy wheelchair rides and reasons to smile and, most important, to give love.

Then, in 1987, the state moved Michael to an institution for children—one that was 320 miles away from Newman. Three days later, this caring man moved that distance, too, so that he could be there for Michael. "I felt like I needed to come," Newman told a reporter. And he was right, for in the short time that the two friends were separated, Michael had become despondent. That changed as soon as his loving friend arrived.

Since that time, Newman has devoted his life to Michael. "I gained as much out of it as he did," Newman said. "Anyone who looks after children gains from it. I think it keeps me feeling better. I feel like I've got something to give him." He certainly does have something to give this boy: unconditional love.

Upon being widowed, Newman could have wallowed in a state of loneliness. Instead, he chose to go out of his way for someone in need, and he's benefited from his actions. I realize that what Mr. Newman has done is not what many of us are able to do. But every day, we can make small gestures of kindness. Starting tomorrow, go out of your way for at least two people each day. You'll soon see the benefits of these gestures come back to you.

2. Have a Plan for Each Day. When you're lonely and think you have nothing to look forward to, your loneliness is going to seem amplified. The antidote is to have a flexible plan for each day.

Each morning, make a list of things to do. Always include activities that will put you in contact with at least two other people even if the contact is over the phone. As often as possible, plan outings to inexpensive public places you enjoy: a favorite park, a museum or library. Check the newspaper for free concerts, plays, meetings of groups or clubs that might interest you. Get involved with your church's activities. If you're an avid bridge player, see if there's a local bridge club. If you pursue an interest, you'll meet other people who share this interest. It's much easier to make new friends when you already have a common bond.

Because I have been working outside of my home all these years, I, like many women, have lost contact with friends I had years ago. Since it's not always easy being sociable when you come home tired from a job, I've set a goal to invite a friend or loved one to lunch at least once a week. Perhaps you could do the same. If you're blessed by knowing several people whose company you relish, set up a standing engagement to meet with each individual on specific days every month.

You can also give yourself something to look forward to each day by taking the following step.

3. Make Yourself Interesting to Yourself. Spending time alone can be a wonderful experience. We all need to be alone once in a while, for it is while we're alone that we can work on ourselves. Even Jesus needed solitude on more than one occasion. And He always seemed to seek it out when He needed to pray or work through a problem.

Making the most of our time alone allows us to make ourselves interesting to ourselves. During these quiet personal times, we can draw closer to God, we can do some soul-searching, we can read a book that enriches our lives. We can help our personalities flourish.

Norman often advised people suffering from loneliness to keep their personalities alive. "You do not want to let the lamp go out," he wrote. "How can you expect to make an impression, to captivate and stimulate, unless you keep that personality spark alive?"

If you're lonely, you should also do a self-examination of your personality. Is there something about the way you behave that repels people? Do you act kindly toward others, or do you easily lose your patience? Are you quick to criticize? Such was the case of a woman who consulted Norman.

This woman, Ruth, didn't have a friend. She would go home after work, cook dinner, then go to bed. She vigorously insisted to Norman that the real cause of her loneliness was her difficulty in making friends in a large city.

When Norman delved a little deeper into her personality, he found that she was highly critical of everyone she knew. He also found out that her past roommate had terminated their living arrangement when Ruth didn't do her share of the housework or meet her share of the expenses.

The more Norman looked into this woman's childhood, the more problems he found. He helped her to understand why she was so hypercritical of others. Slowly, her attitudes changed. Hesitantly, she became involved in her church. Then she joined a drama club. Her new interests led to new acquaintances and, eventually, to new friends. All of this was brought about when she learned that her loneliness was the result of her attitudes toward others.

Do you project a friendly air? If not, act as if you are friendly. I'm a firm believer in the "as-if" principle Norman often suggested. If you continuously act a certain way, this behavior becomes reality. Acting friendly is simply showing an interest in another person. It doesn't take much to warmly greet someone and take the time to listen to what he has to say.

4. Call on Your Closest Friend and Your Memories. I've been doing my greatest battles with loneliness in the evenings, when I'm away from my work and family. This is when I spend my most precious time with my closest friend, Jesus. I talk with Him about things that occurred during the day, much the way Norman and I used to talk. If I have a problem, I go over it with Him. Invariably, if I listen carefully, a wise answer comes.

I'm afraid this will sound like a cliche, but it's really not: Jesus is your friend. You are never alone. He is there whenever you need Him. Jesus told His disciples, "Behold, I am with you always, even to the end of the age" (Matthew 28:20). Take this promise to heart.

In times of loneliness, I also find myself calling upon my memories of Norman. We had a wonderful life together, and reminding myself of it makes me more grateful to God.

If you're lonely because a loved one is absent from your life, write a letter to him or her. Thank this person for the specific blessings he brought to your life. Pour your heart into this letter, recalling all of the good times you had together. Then re-read it as often as you need to. Let this letter be a reminder of how good God has been to you.

There you have it, my battle plan for loneliness. Now that you have the strategies, let's win this war together. There's no need for any of us to feel lonely again.

Joy is not in things; it is in us. —*Anonymous*

CHAPTER 2

Simplify Your Life

Whoever does not receive the kingdom of God as a little child will by no means enter it. —Luke 18:17

"LESS is more," wrote poet Robert Browning. I can attest to that. From personal experience, I can tell you that a simplified life is much more relaxing and enjoyable. It took me quite a few years to reach the point where I was willing to simplify, but now that I've begun to do so, it is a glorious feeling. Here are three easy things you can do.

1. Ask Yourself, "What's Really Important?" What are your overall priorities? Financial success? An enduring relationship with your family? An immaculate house? Economic security for your heirs? Before you can begin living simply, you have to make these determinations. And once you've established what is really important, you'll be able to let go of those things that aren't.

How does one do this? Begin by creating your own personal mission statement: a sentence or paragraph that sums up simply what you want your priorities to be. For example, a man I spoke with recently described his this way: "My ultimate goal is to make all of my relationships, whether with God, my family or the butcher, strong, giving, and positive. I never want anything of a materialistic nature to stand in the way of any of my relationships."

I admire the mission statement this man lives by. When one establishes a clear-cut set of rules, it becomes easier to live a simple life. For instance, the man I've just mentioned will never allow the lure of money, a job promotion, or a slick sports car to stand in the way of his relationships as long as he sticks with his mission.

For a long time, there has been a disturbing trend in this country—one that I hope will subside. That trend is the undue emphasis we place upon material possessions. We seem to feel that by accumulating things, we will be secure. We are somewhat like children who, while in bed, surround themselves with all their favorite toys to feel secure. We adults might look at them, and ask, "How can they sleep, surrounded by so much clutter?" But, in our own way, are we any different?

Now, I believe that enough money in the bank to pay your bills is a good thing. I also believe that a person should accumulate whatever material goods is consistent with his or her best life. And I see no inconsistency in good, solid free enterprise, provided we also have good, solid spiritual thinking and sharing. But one has to keep everything in balance. Otherwise, material possessions become more important than anything else.

Here is a touching and affirming example of one man who knew how to keep everything in balance. And, after you've read his story, consider how you may have reacted under similar circumstances.

Norman and I knew a man who owned a magnificent home high up in the hills of California. Upon hearing that a devastating fire destroyed many of the luxury homes in our friend's part of the state, Norman immediately called him.

When he finally reached our friend, Norman found out that within one hour of the blaze reaching this man's house, it had burned to the ground. "We are sorry you lost your house," Norman tried to console our friend.

He, in turn, replied, "Don't you and Ruth worry about us. Jane and the kids are safe and our family is together. The house was only a possession. We struggled for it and we built it and we certainly enjoyed it, but we are safe and that's what counts."

The admiration Norman and I felt for this man grew even stronger after this incident. He could have bemoaned his bad luck. But instead, he dwelt upon what was truly important to him—his family's safety.

As you consider what is really important, you will be preparing yourself to take this next important step.

2. Give It Away. I've already mentioned that it's difficult to live amid clutter. By this, I mean two types of clutter: the kind we hold in our brain and what we surround ourselves with. The two often go hand-in-hand. Notice how hard it is to focus on a task when everything around you is a mess. Now, put yourself in an orderly, simple environment. You'll immediately think sharper, less jumbled thoughts. To really understand the beauty of uncluttered simplicity, visit a Quaker church. In that setting, you'll truly appreciate how sparseness frees up your ability to think.

The clutter we hold in our brain can be anything from negative thoughts to a list of things we must accomplish within the next eight hours. It's clutter all the same. The clutter around us can be piles of old publications that we're hanging on to "just in case," or a valuable, lovely, but overwhelming collection of antique vases.

This is all clutter we can either get rid of or reduce. To get started, go through your house and throw out anything you don't need and can't recycle. Examine some of your treasured possessions. Is there something you own that you know one of your grown children would appreciate? If so, pass it on. I did this recently with many of the possessions Norman and I had accumulated over the years. Luckily, I have a large family, so those things that held a tremendous sentimental value to me are staying within our family. And, I have to tell you, it was a joyful experience to see how pleased my children and grandchildren were to receive these items.

Another satisfying benefit of giving things away is that my household is now more organized!

If you aren't ready to give away some of the possessions you value, try storing them in a safe place. Once in a while, take the stored items out, redecorate with them, and place the more recently used items away for future use.

Once you've worked on your environment, it will be much easier for you to rid yourself of mind clutter, for you will already feel more organized. But if the mind clutter persists, take a look at your personal mission statement. What is causing the confusion in your mind? Perhaps your lifestyle is not consistent with your mission. Are you overwhelmed by too many commitments? If this is the case, you must learn to say "no" to the extra tasks you don't have to do. Also, don't be shy about delegating some of your workload to others in your family. And by all means, if you have a big job ahead of you that would be more quickly and better done by a professional, hire one.

3. Simplify Your Faith. Among the wisest advice and caution you can find in the Bible is the following: "Whoever does not receive the kingdom of God as a little child will by no means enter it" (Luke 18:17). In other words, you are to live your faith and to believe in God with the innocence and acceptance with which a child views a parent. Don't complicate your faith by questioning God's authority.

Here's something Norman wrote that I think you'll benefit from:

> Christianity deals with vast realities, but it does so in an uncomplicated way. I have been re-reading the Gospels and letters of Saint Paul. There is where you find out what Christianity really is. Go back to the sources—the Gospels and Saint Paul. In my reading, I've noticed that there are four words that stand out. In the New Testament, the word righteousness occurs 100 times; the word truth, 120; life; 185 times, love, 210 times. The simple teaching of Christian faith is that of righteousness, truth, life, and love. Those are the four words that give us the simple essence of what Jesus taught.

Pretty straightforward, isn't it? So why do we attempt to muddle our faith by over analyzing it? From what I've seen, those who view themselves as sophisticated, worldly people are those who make faith so complicated and philosophical they wind up abandoning it. Faith for these people becomes too difficult.

Here's the story of a couple who had such an experience.

> One beautiful autumn day, a couple we barely knew drove up to our house in Pawling. They had come from New York City to seek Norman's counsel. It seems the man was greatly troubled because he and his wife weren't getting any satisfaction out of life. They had money and power and had made a name for themselves in society. But none of this was enough.

"Mary is sick nearly all of the time," he said. "As for me, I'm as miserable as can be. We don't feel as though we're making our lives count for anything. We thought you could help us."

Norman glanced at the couple. "Frankly," he said, "you may be too sophisticated and complicated for my simple ways. Your approach to life seems so superficial. But I can tell you where you can get the help you need. My advice to you is that you both immerse your minds in the Bible." Doubting that the couple owned a Bible, he pulled one of ours off the shelf and handed it to them. "Begin your reading with the Psalms and the four gospels—Matthew, Mark, Luke, and John—and then Paul's letters to the Romans, the Corinthians, and the Galatians," he advised. "Saturate your minds with this book. If you do this—really do it—you will make valuable, life-changing discoveries."

After the couple left, Norman confided in me that he was skeptical as to whether they would do what he suggested, but I sensed a desperation in this couple. I had a feeling they truly wanted something deeper than what money was buying them.

As it turned out, they were ready to try simple faith. A few months later, Norman received a note from the husband. "Never have I had such a springtime," he wrote. "Never has the grass seemed greener. Never have I had so much joy in living. And Mary's health is so much better that she's a different person." His concluding words were direct: "God has come into our lives."

The best of luck to you as you begin your journey toward a simpler life.

Simplicity, carried to an extreme, becomes elegance.

—Jon Franklin

CHAPTER 3

Keep Your Principles Strong—No Matter What

No good thing will he with-hold from them that walk uprightly. —*Psalm 84:11*

W HAT a time we are living in! On any given day, we hear about powerful, well-known figures whose actions are less than exemplary. The temptations that go along with positions of power in our society appear to be too great for some people to handle. Each day, we also read or hear about shocking, senseless acts committed by seemingly "normal" people: young children neglected, abused, murdered; acts of terror committed in the name of religion; random violence running rampant throughout our nation's cities, towns, and our once safe countryside.

Sadly, within our own communities and our own circles of friends and acquaintances, we also hear of destructive behavior: marital infidelity, drug abuse, fraud. We seem to be surrounded by corruption in one form or another. We must guard ourselves against even the smallest aspect of it, otherwise this behavior will knock us down and steal our self-respect. Here are three courses of action we can take to protect and maintain our principles.

1. Get Back to Basics. As children, most of us were taught right from wrong. The basics of the Christian moral code were given to us when we were admonished not to cheat, lie, lust for, envy or hurt others. But sometimes those basic teachings become a little fuzzy. For example, a store clerk mistakenly undercharges you for an item. Do you point out the mistake or do you happily walk away, considering yourself lucky? If you choose the latter, aren't you cheating and hurting another by allowing the store clerk to answer for the mistake? In your conscience, so will you. Here's another example: Your closest friend has just purchased the house of your dreams. Are you happy that your friend has found such a beautiful home or do you find yourself envying her good fortune? Finally, it's a beautiful early summer day, but you have no vacation time left. You'd love to stay home to enjoy the pleasant weather. Do you call your boss to report that you're feeling ill?

It is the little transgressions in life that we have to be on the lookout for. How do we do that? By getting back to the basics. We all know the Ten Commandments and many can probably recite them. But how often do we really apply them to the ordinary situations in our lives? When you finish reading this chapter, take a new look at them. Question whether you have been applying the principles of the Ten Commandments to the situations you face on a daily basis. This foundation upon which our moral code was built can be found in Deuteronomy 5:7-21.

After you've reviewed the Ten Commandments, don't put your Bible away on the bookshelf. Instead, place it where you can see it, perhaps on a table next to your favorite chair. If you read in bed, put your Bible on your nightstand. Make a pact with yourself that you'll read the Bible for a few minutes each evening before you pick up another book. Part of getting back to the basics includes going back to good, old-fashioned Bible reading. Five or ten minutes spent with this Book is an excellent way to gird up your values.

Keeping your Bible in view will also serve as a visual reminder that you can stand tall and feel clean in a world that is sometimes tarnished with greed, ugliness, and dishonesty. Take a few moments to think of other inspiring visual reminders that you can place strategically around your house or office. Does looking at a painting of Jesus fill you with peace? Does a simple cross on a wall inspire you to stay in touch with your faith? Even a newspaper clipping or a magazine article about someone who has behaved morally and valiantly might prompt you to do the same.

In the book *Chicken Soup for the Soul at Work,* a contributor shared one man's experience, which clearly illustrates the importance of positive visual reminders.

Dennis J. McCauley was having car trouble. The garage

he usually used had gone out of business. Like most of us facing car problems, he wasn't happy about going to a new, unknown mechanic. But upon a friend's recommendation, he gave a shop called "D's Auto Repair" a try.

While inside the shop's office, he noticed a framed newspaper article on the wall. The headline caught his attention. "Local Dairy Farmer Kills Whole Herd," it read. Upon reading the article, McCauley learned that there had been a tainted milk scare in Michigan that was attributed to diseased cows. When officials decided to have all of the cows in Michigan tested, the dairy industry protested and a legal tangle followed. Until it could be straightened out, the dairy farmers were to proceed with business as usual. But there was one dairy farmer who couldn't go on with business until he knew that his herd was healthy. At his own expense, he had his cows tested. Only a few had the disease, but there was a possibility that the entire herd could be infected. So the farmer had the whole herd killed and buried. He didn't want to risk producing tainted beef or milk. The financial loss was entirely his to bear. Insurance would have covered the loss only if the state had mandated the slaughter. Even so, when a reporter asked the farmer why he did it, he replied, "Because it was the right thing to do."

McCauley questioned the shop's owner about the significance of the framed article. The mechanic told McCauley that the farmer inspired him by setting a standard for integrity that he wanted to live up to. And, as McCauley developed a relationship with his new mechanic, he discovered that the man did indeed live up to the basic standard he set for himself: high integrity.

Keep your eyes open for stories that will inspire you to be your best. Keep a scrapbook of them. Then, when you're feeling less than dedicated, review the articles. This exercise will also help you in the next course of action.

2. Be True to What You Believe. Sometimes, with all of the confusing messages we receive from the media and other sources, we forget what is vital to our existence. We lose sight of what we really believe in, those basic ingrained values we were brought up with. The luxury car we see advertised on television isn't going to improve our lives, nor will it bring us any closer to God. Having a few extra drinks at a dinner party will not make anyone more charming, so why run the risk of damaging your health or your reputation? And is that promotion worth making your competing co-worker look bad?

Always be true to the values you fundamentally believe in. This takes courage and strength, but the payoff is worth it, because you will become a person of honor to others, to yourself and, most important, to God.

With Ken Blanchard, Norman wrote a book entitled *The Power of Ethical Management.* It contains a helpful list of affirmations that can aid you in making sure you are being true to your values. Here is a condensed version of what Norman and Ken called "The Five Principles of Ethical Power":

Purpose: I let my conscience be my guide. No matter what, I am always able to face the mirror, look myself straight in the eye, and feel good about myself.

Pride: A balanced self-esteem keeps my ego and my desire to be accepted from influencing my decisions.

Patience: I believe that things will eventually work out well. I don't need everything to happen right now.

Persistence: I stick to my purpose, especially when it seems inconvenient to do so.

Perspective: I take time to enter each day quietly in a mood of reflection. This helps me to get myself focused and to see more clearly.

Here's an affirmation of my own, one that doesn't begin with the letter "P." It is:

Faithfulness: I honor and abide by the rules God has set forth, knowing that my soul will someday benefit from this faithfulness, for "no good thing will he withhold from them that walk uprightly" (Psalm 84:11).

Use these affirmations each day until they become ingrained in your consciousness.

3. See Temptation's Opportunity. Peter Marshall, one of the most inspiring Christian communicators of the 20th century, said that there is no sin in being tempted. It's what we decide to do about the temptation that counts. "Temptation," he said, "is an opportunity to conquer."

Temptation comes to all of us, but, as Norman said time and again, we have the spiritual weapons for gaining victory over it. An insightful piece of wisdom regarding temptation can be found in Paul's first letter to the Corinthians. We are told that no temptation will ever come to us that has not been faced by others. And if others can overcome it, so can you. God will give you a way out, if you turn to Him and develop a relationship with His Son.

Norman and I knew a young man who faced a tremendous temptation. After struggling and suffering repeated defeats, he turned to Norman for advice. My husband advised the young man to adopt the policy of imaging Jesus walking alongside of him and, when the temptation presented itself, to ask Christ for help in overcoming it. At first, the young man thought this a simple method for tricking his mind, but he did it anyway. Over a brief period, he no longer saw his walks with Jesus as a gimmick. He actually began to feel Jesus' restraining hand upon him. The force of Jesus' tremendous power gave the young man a lasting victory over his temptation.

Try this yourself the next time you're tempted to do something that goes against what you know is right. Imagine Jesus at your side, helping you walk away from temptation. If its destructive magnetism still draws you near, ask Jesus for the power to pull away from the temptation's force.

We can and must live in a sometimes corrupt world without allowing ourselves to become corrupt. And the more we stand up for our values, the more others will take notice and stand up for theirs.

Conscience is a divine voice in the human soul.

—Francis Bowen

CHAPTER 4

Release Your Potential

Not that I have already attained, or am already perfected; but I press on . . . .

—Philippians 3:12

I RECENTLY came across a file of human-interest stories that had been published in newspapers and magazines. As I re-read the articles, I realized the subjects had a common theme: through difficult circumstances, the people featured in the articles were in the process of realizing their potential. Later on in this chapter, I'll tell you about some of these people, but for now, let's do a little soul-searching.

Ask yourself these five questions:

Do I believe I have many great tasks yet to accomplish?
Do I strive each day to reach my potential?
Do I believe that, with God, my potential is limitless?
Do I regularly open my mind to new experiences?
Do the people around me believe in me?

I hope that you have answered "yes" to each of these questions. To be honest, not even I, someone who lives and breathes positive thinking principles, can answer each affirmatively.

But I firmly believe that, with God at our side, our possibilities are limitless! Here are three steps you can take to help uncover and release your potential.

1. View Yourself as an Unfinished Masterpiece. You are a great artistic achievement. Although you are incomplete, God and you are the collaborating artists, putting on the finishing touches: the subtle tones of wisdom that experience brings, the glow in your eyes that faith brings, the confident posture that success brings.

Each day, the masterpiece that is you requires additional improvement. There may be occasions when the masterpiece doesn't seem to be coming together, but let those days fade from your memory. Start each day fresh with a new, positive attitude. And remind yourself, on any bad day, of the personal insight Paul wrote of to the Philippians: "Not that I have already attained, or am already perfected; but I press on, that I may lay hold of that for which I also was laid hold of by Jesus Christ" (Philippians 3:12).

I've met and heard of many works in progress. Sometimes, it takes more than the artistic hands of God and the subject to help complete the masterpiece (which is why it's important to surround yourself with people who believe in your potential). I remember Norman telling me of one particular incident in which the potential of one of God's masterpieces was nearly recklessly destroyed.

A dear friend of Norman's managed a Chicago hotel. Norman stayed there often. One time at the hotel, while speaking at a barbers' convention, Norman learned that the attending barbers had gone down to Madison Street and found a drunk lying on the sidewalk. One barber took a photo of the man. They then proceeded to clean him up, giving him a haircut and manicure, along with a new suit, shoes, shirt, and tie. After his physical transformation was complete, the barber took another photo. Thus the man became Exhibit A at the convention, proof of what barbers could do to change a man.

After the convention, the barbers paid the man and were about to send him on his way. But Norman's friend Gus, the hotel manager, wondered what was to become of this man. He, like Norman, had a heart filled with love. Gus talked to the man: "You can make something of your life. I'll get you a job, but don't let me down. I have faith in you."

The man assured Gus he wouldn't let him down. A job followed and the man showed up for three days. But on the fourth, he was nowhere to be seen. Gus went to Madison Street and found the man drunk, lying on newspapers. He then brought him back to the hotel and talked to him. "All the barbers can do is fix a person on the outside," Gus said. "But I've got a Friend who works on the inside. His name is Jesus. If you let Him do on the inside what the barbers did on the outside, you'll be somebody!"

It was a tough journey for Gus, and for the man whose failure was deeply imbedded in his subconscious. But Gus stayed with him, believing in his potential, until the man found Jesus. Once this man began viewing himself as God's masterpiece, he became a sober, hardworking, reliable human being. He also returned Gus's tremendous favor by performing similar acts of faith to others who were downtrodden.

Norman once wrote that the genius of Christianity is how it changes people. How it takes weak people and makes them strong, how it takes mean people and makes them loving, how it takes ineffective people and makes them productive and competent.

I agree. Your faith in God and Jesus Christ is your most powerful tool in completing the masterpiece you are meant to be.

2. Get More Out of Life. To explore your potential, you have to begin getting more out of life. Shutting yourself up in your own little world won't allow you to test your abilities and interests.

I read of an 80-year-old man who kept a detailed diary of everything he had done each hour of every day for most of his life. By studying this diary, he calculated the use he had made of his time. This is what he came up with: He had spent 26 years sleeping, 21 years working, 228 days shaving and 140 days paying bills! He also spent more than 26 days scolding his children and two days yelling at his dogs. Only 26 hours were devoted to laughing. You notice, he didn't note how much time he spent in church. Perhaps, if he had been there more, his life wouldn't have seemed so bleak.

Well, it's not too late, even for this man, to uncover life's possibilities, but the leap must be taken. Seize the day, this day and every day that God grants you.

In the file I referred to before, one of the inspiring stories I came across was the account of Stanley Gould, a man whose potential could have lay buried had he not explored all that life has to offer.

At 41, Stanley Gould easily could have excused himself from trying to reach his potential. Cerebral palsy had caused his limbs to twist and his speech to slur. But, instead of laying back and doing nothing, he filled in as a volunteer assistant basketball coach at the local school. He was so good at what he did that when the school's head coach quit, Stanley was able to fill the position. Then, along with coaching, he began helping out in the school's computer lab. And when the local library needed board members, Stanley volunteered again.

This is a perfect example of a man who is constantly broadening his horizons to achieve his potential. And although he is wheelchair -bound, his spirit is not bound to anything. "It's all for the kids," he told a reporter. "I can stay home and feel sorry for myself, or I can be active and be happy."

The school principal says that Stanley has an uncanny ability to counsel young people. "They know that if he can do difficult things, they can find a way to do them, too. The kids' grades have improved and so has their behavior," said the principal. "Stanley is not only a great role model, he also gives these youngsters the drive they need to continue on with life."

Because Stanley Gould opened himself up to new experiences, he has uncovered his potential, and is positively touching the lives of young people. And, based on what I've read about him, Stanley will continue to seek out new challenges each day.

How can you begin to get more out of life so that you can unleash your potential? I recommend that you pursue or learn about everything that even vaguely interests you. If, as a child, you wanted piano lessons, but never had them, start now. If you have a concern about this country's illiteracy problem, become a tutor.

If you love to write or paint, take a course. There's a world of opportunity out there for you each day. Take advantage of it!

3. Be Alert. To live each day to the fullest, you have to be alert. This means plenty of sleep, exercise, and healthy habits. Don't be like the football player I recently read about in Carl Mays' book *A Strategy for Winning*. The player approached his coach and said, "I've got to do something. My stomach is getting so big I can't even look down and see my big toe."

Glancing at the boy, the coach said. "You need to diet."

"What?" the player asked.

"Diet." the coach repeated.

"Oh," the player replied, "what color?"

Get it? Dye it. I just thought I'd throw that in to explore my potential as a comedienne. I think I'll stick to writing. But you get the point. Our minds don't work properly unless we take care of our bodies and souls.

Norman knew a man who spent his latter years uncovering his potential. A successful 80-year-old businessman, Bill looked no more than 35 years old. His personality was warm, outgoing, and his alertness to the world around him was astounding.

Norman asked Bill how he managed to stay in such good physical and mental shape. His answer:

> "For years, I treated my body abominably. But now that I have dedicated myself to God, I treat my body with reverence. I sleep eight hours every night, and before I go to bed, I check my worries with God; I forgive everyone; and then I get into bed and say, 'Lord, I am your child; now give Thy beloved sleep.' And I let my body relax. I've also stopped doing things that will take away my vigor. I watch my diet, I stopped smoking and I don't touch liquor any more.
>
> "I've learned to keep in harmony with God," Bill continued. "Every morning, I affirm the good; I affirm health and wellbeing; I affirm the teachings of Christ; I affirm the Lord as love, joy and truth; I affirm service to others as my goal."

Bill was an expert at uncovering and unleashing his potential. He fully understood and lived the ideas I've just written about, viewing himself as God's masterpiece. You, too, should see yourself in this light. Go ahead, make some bold strokes and unleash the best of yourself! Your potential as a work of art is unlimited.

Life consists not in holding good cards, but in playing well those you hold.

—Josh Billings

CHAPTER 5

Bounce Back From From Disappointment

And we know that all things work together for good to those who love God.

—Romans 8:28

HAVE you recently been disappointed? The answer is probably yes. We all deal with disappointment. I could cite at least five disappointments that I've had just in the last week. I guess you could say it was a tough week! Since disappointments touch all our lives, we need to learn how to rebound from them. Our ability to gracefully bounce back from disappointment, and be philosophical about it, is a mark of our maturity as positive thinkers. Here are three disappointment-quashing methods I've practiced over the years.

1. Let Go of Your Anger and Resentment. Watch how some children handle disappointment. They pout, stamp their feet, even cry when things don't go their way. They haven't learned that disappointment is fleeting, so they get angry and frustrated. Sadly, many adults behave the same way. I've been angered by disappointments in my life. And I've had to consciously reason myself out of that anger. You can do the same.

What good does it do to lash out at loved ones, friends or co-workers when we suffer a setback? When disappointment comes, let go of the nonproductive feelings you have: anger, frustration, resentment, self-hate, depression. Use the energy you might spend on these emotions to do something constructive, something that will take your mind off your defeat and put you on the road to victory.

Norman had a favorite saying that went like this: "Never chew your pills; swallow them, for chewing them makes them more bitter still." He often shared it with people who came to him embittered by life's blows. I remember him telling me about a young man to whom he gave this quote.

This man was full of anger, hate and resentment because, after having worked at a company for a number of years, he was passed up for a promotion that he worked hard to attain. He felt he had been double-crossed, and went into great detail about the man he felt had double-crossed him. "I have lost my faith in the integrity of top management," he told Norman.

Norman asked the man if he had found another position. "As a matter of fact," he said, "I now have a better job. With my old company, the promotion I should have been given was the last I could have gotten; it was a dead end. Where I am now, while I don't make as much money, the opportunities are practically unlimited. I really see a future for myself."

When Norman asked him why he was still angry after everything worked out, the man said: "I did not deserve the treatment I got. Suppose someone treated you like that?"

Norman tried to help this man let go of his resentment, and to see that he had done well, but the man seemed to want to wallow in his anger. He let his emotions cloud any possibility of clearly and reasonably seeing the good that came out of his situation.

Don't let this happen to you. When disappointments come, let go of your negative emotions before they steal precious time from you. How can you do this? I know a simple, yet effective, technique. I've learned to pray those feelings away. I've found that if I talk to God about the negative feelings I have, no matter how ugly, they vanish.

Once you rid yourself of your negative thoughts, you are ready for the next step.

2. Open Yourself to God's Will. One of my favorite Bible verses is Romans 8:28: "And we know that all things work together for good to those who love God, to those who are the called according to his purpose." This verse was also one of Norman's favorites. Norman wrote:

"When disappointed, try loving God all the more. Carefully analyze yourself to make certain you are thinking and living in harmony with His spiritual purpose. It could be that you are off the spiritual beam. Instead of dwelling upon the word "disappointment," think of it as "Hisappointment." What you regard as a disappointment may actually be His plan.

"Always take a positive view toward disappointment. Maybe you are being led toward something different. If you have tried sincerely and prayerfully and things have not gone well, then look upon disappointment as an opportunity to ask whether you should move, under God's guidance, in another direction."

What Norman refers to requires us to have a philosophical view of disappointment. We knew a woman who developed that type of view, and who ended up content with what God had in mind for her.

Norman and I were being entertained in the home of this woman and her husband. They showed us around their house, an old place they had fixed over and were proud of. "You are a marvelous housekeeper," Norman said to the wife.

"That is a compliment to me now," she said, "but there was a time when I wouldn't have thought so. As a girl, I wanted a career. I studied hard in college, and graduated with honors. Then I looked around for fields to conquer. 'I'll teach,' I decided. So I thought I'd make a great name for myself as a teacher.

"Then I learned to pray about my life, not to try to force things according to my own wishes. I told the Lord I would do anything He wanted me to do. And in about two weeks, I met a young, struggling doctor who hadn't two nickels to his name. I thought he was wonderful, and pretty soon we were married. Finally, we got this house. Would you like to see some samples of my career?"

She took us upstairs into three successive bedrooms, and there lay three beautiful, tousled heads on their pillows. "Aren't they sweet?" she said.

We went on through the house and finally ended up in the kitchen. Over each appliance hung a different document. Over one was her college diploma, above another her certificate to teach. "These," she said, "are the marks of this career woman."

This woman wanted one thing, but the Lord wanted something else for her, so she adjusted herself to God's will. And, it turned out, God's choice was one she thoroughly enjoyed.

We should all learn to ask God, "What do you want me to do?" Anyone who constantly and persistently does that will see his or her way through disappointments. Open yourself up to God. Adjust yourself to His will, and He will lead you down paths you might never have considered.

3. Wait and Watch—The Good Will Come. After you have become philosophical about handling your disappointments, you'll be ready to observe the mysterious ways in which God works. His plans for us sometimes become most evident after the harshest disappointments. I'll never forget how unhappy and resentful I was when I had to postpone a year of college in order for my brother to complete his education. At the time, I couldn't have dreamed that anything good would come out of that. But my future hinged on the delay, because without it I would never have met Norman. I would almost certainly have left Syracuse before he arrived!

Waiting for the good to come out of a disappointment requires patience and trust in God. A friend who faced a horrible blow proved to Norman and me just how much trust and patience are required.

This man, at the age of 54, found himself unemployed when the company he worked for went bankrupt. Sadly, many companies won't even consider hiring someone his age. Most people I've known reached their most productive years in their 50s. Everywhere our friend turned, his age worked against him.

When we learned of his situation, Norman went to see him, expecting to find him depressed. But he surprised Norman by saying, "God is trying to say something, so I'm practicing being quiet, and I'm looking for light from on high." You see, our friend was a trusting believer in Jesus' promises. He had saturated his mind with the Bible's wisdom. When adversity and disappointment came, he was not overwhelmed.

Eighteen months of futile job searching passed. Then an executive of a great service organization came to our friend and said, "We have a vacancy in our organization, the number four position, and we think you are a natural for it." The next time we saw him, he remarked, "This job never would have come to me if I had not had the trouble first."

Our friend was happier in this job than he'd ever been. Throughout his search for employment, he held to the idea that God had something special planned for him, and He did. Look back on the times that you were disappointed, even devastated by a situation. Make a list of these incidents. Then think back to the good that came out of being led down a different path. Across from your disappointment, list the benefits that followed. Let's say you were disappointed when you weren't accepted into a particular college. Instead, you went to one where you met friends that you still have today. That qualifies as a benefit. Add to this list when new disappointments come into your life. Then, as soon as you recognize the benefit, jot that down.

One final suggestion: Read and commit to memory the Twenty-third Psalm. When disappointments come, comfort yourself with the knowledge that God's plan for you is good, and you will ultimately see why He has chosen certain paths for you to follow. May you be able to see "Hisappointments" in all of your disappointments.

The greatest mistake anyone can make is to be afraid of making one.

—Elbert Hubbard

CHAPTER 6

Give Yourself The Gift of Worry-Less Living

I sought the Lord, and he heard me, and delivered me from all my fears.

—Psalm 34:13

I'M NOT USUALLY a worrier, but even I sometimes find myself caught in the trap of worrying whether I'll be able to do all that needs to be done. I don't like to worry. I'm sure none of us does, but many times we get caught off guard by this negative state of mind. When we let our defenses down, worry sneaks into our brain, feeding it the worst possible scenarios.

I heard of one mother who expects to hear from her grown son every night, because she worries about him as he travels the roads as a truck driver. The evenings that she doesn't receive a phone call from him, she panics, imagining the worst has happened. This is a horrible way to live! Worry dominates this woman's life. She isn't taking advantage of the most basic principles of Christianity that lead to worry-less living. Let's look at those principles.

1. Why Worry When You Can Pray? Norman and I once knew a clown named Happy, whom we kept in touch with over the years.

> One time when Norman asked Happy how he was doing, the clown replied, "Well, you know how it is. We all have our ups and downs, the bitter with the sweet."
>
> "I hope you're not worrying about anything," Norman said.
>
> "Of course not," Happy replied. "Why worry when you can pray?"

This struck Norman and me as a sound philosophy toward this tendency to worry. If we could each day say to ourselves, *Why worry when I can pray?* we would eventually get worry under control.

Praying dispels worry in two ways. First, it releases and activates your built-in strength—the often untapped strength God has given you. You pray the strength out, you believe it out, you practice it out. And then the worry fades away. In Psalm 34:13, we read, "I sought the Lord, and he heard me, and delivered me from all my fears." Memorize this incredible statement, for it speaks of a miracle that can occur in your life.

The second thing prayer does is teach you to think—and that eliminates worry. So many of us don't really think. Praying activates the mind so that you can understand, you get increased know-how and new perceptions, you become more alert, more in tune with God's wisdom. All of this, in turn, gives you power over worry.

I remember reading of a 28-year-old pilot who was flying a little pontoon plane in northwestern Ontario. His adventure points up the value of praying instead of worrying.

This young man was out scouting an isolated little lake, far from civilization. After setting his plane down onto the lake, he stepped out of the cockpit and onto one of the pontoons. The propeller was still turning. He slipped, hitting his head, and toppled unconscious into the water.

The cold water revived him, and he grabbed a pontoon. Then he discovered, to his horror, that the propeller had cut off his right arm just below the shoulder, and he was bleeding profusely.

There he was—far from civilization, in a lake, his arm cut off, blood pouring out of him. What would you or I do? Worry? That surely wouldn't do any good, would it?

What did he do? He prayed. And he got an answer. He managed to pull himself up onto the pontoon and into the cockpit. He fastened a tourniquet around his bleeding stump. He did what he had to do to lift the plane off the water. All the time praying that he would not black out, he flew fifteen miles to another lake, where he got help.

Apparently, everyone was astonished by the amazing power this man had over himself. But he was a man of prayer, and he found that prayer gave him power; whereas worry, in that crisis, would have destroyed him.

Perhaps we've never faced a situation this harrowing. I hope none of us ever does. But we've all been up against situations which, because of their importance to us individually, needed all the power we could summon. Don't ever say to yourself, "I can't handle it." You can handle anything. With God, you are greater than you think. Why worry when you can pray?

To get yourself started on praying instead of worrying, write down your worries. One by one, pray to God about them, explaining the situation. Then surrender the worry to God. Tell Him that the outcome is in His hands, and that you'll accept His will in the matter. The more you do this, the less the burden of worry will dominate your life.

2. Learn To Relax. Worry seems to go hand-in-hand with a person's inability to relax. I have never met a worrier who wasn't also a victim of tension. When you pray, as I have suggested above, you become calm and confident. You have tranquility, so tension dies. When you're free from tension and your mind is clear, there isn't anything you can't handle.

Norman wrote the following suggestions for relaxing one's mind, where worry dwells.

> While sitting relaxed in a chair, think of your mind as the surface of a lake in a storm, tossed by waves and in tumult. But now the waves subside, and the surface of the lake is placid and unruffled.
>
> Spend two or three minutes thinking of the most beautiful and peaceful scenes you have ever beheld. For example, a mountain at sunset, or a deep valley filled with the hush of early morning, or moonlight upon rippling waters. Go back in your memory and relive these scenes.
>
> Bringing out the melody in each, slowly repeat a series of words that expresses quietness and peace. For example, tranquility, serenity, quietness. Think of other such words and repeat them.

Make a mental list of times in your life when you have been conscious of God's watchful care, and recall how, when you were worried, He brought things out right and took care of you. Then repeat this verse from an old hymn, "So long Thy power hath blest me, sure it still will lead me on."

Now repeat the following words, which have an amazing power to relax the mind: "Thou wilt keep him in perfect peace whose mind is stayed on Thee." Repeat this three times.

At several times during the day, whenever you have a moment, repeat that Scripture verse, out loud if possible, so that by the end of the day you will have said it many times. Conceive of these words as active, vital ingredients permeating your mind, sending into every area of your thinking a healing balm. This is the best medicine known to man for taking tension out of the mind.

With prayer and the above relaxation techniques, our tensions will slow down along with the amount of worrying we do.

3. Take Things as They Come. In my preparations for dealing with both personal and professional commitments, I've developed several lists of things I need to do. But no matter how many lists one has, no matter how well prepared someone is, the uncontrollable comes up. For instance, let's say you're planning to buy your grandson Power Rangers for his birthday, or some other toy, something he believes he cannot live without. When you get to the store, you find that this item is sold out, and is also not available in any store in the area. Do you panic, do you lose sleep, worrying that little Johnny will be disappointed? The answer is no. You just take things as they come, and do your best at picking a suitable substitute gift.

The great industrialist Henry Ford once gave someone his philosophy of life: "I have a few simple rules," he said, "for I am essentially a simple man. First, I do not eat too much. Second, I do not worry too much. Third, I put my faith in God and do my best and believe that whatever happens is for the best."

This same philosophy was held by a prominent magazine editor who said, "I plan well, I work hard. I leave nothing to be taken for granted. I pray about it. If someone disappoints me, if something goes awry and doesn't work out the way I want, I try to be philosophical, for there is nothing I can do."

These two people shared the important skill of taking things as they come. Perhaps it is best illustrated by a story I once heard.

There was a Chinese gentleman who had tied a pot of soup to one end of a pole. He was walking along with this earthen crock over his shoulder when it fell off the pole and smashed into pieces. Without even looking back, he kept right on walking. Someone said to him, "Your crock is broken and your soup is gone. Why don't you stop and do something about it?"

He said, "What can I do about it? The crock is broken and the soup is spilt. I might as well keep going."

How many of us would take that attitude? We would most likely fret and be in a great dither about the broken crock. What we have to remember is that there's no sense in worrying over past failures, present situations, or potential mishaps. As long as we truly do our best as positive-thinking Christians, God will see that we get our ultimate reward.

Blessed is the person too busy to worry in the daytime and too sleepy to worry at night. —Leo Aikman

CHAPTER 7

You Can Gain Power Over Your Weakness

God . . . will not allow you to be tempted beyond what you are able . . . .

—I Corinthians 10:13

W
E ALL HAVE at least one weakness. Some of us might not be able to resist chocolate, others might be addicted to nicotine. Some people can't control their tempers, others are indecisive, some procrastinate. There are a slew of weaknesses that can capture us at any moment, if we aren't careful.

What is your weakness? Do you want to overcome it? If so, carefully follow these three steps.

1. Through Your Weakness, Seek Strength. When we succumb to our weaknesses, most of us wind up berating ourselves afterward. We mimic the alcoholic who swears each morning that he is not going to take another drink, but does so anyway. The following morning, he berates himself, once again swearing to never drink again. There is nothing that lowers our self-esteem faster than letting something that we don't want rule our lives. But on the flip side, the greatest self-esteem booster I can think of is overcoming a weakness.

It takes strength to resist temptations that have become habits. For instance, let us say your weakness is gossip. What if a co-worker tells you he suspects your boss is cheating on his wife? The easy thing for you to do is repeat this tidbit. Think of the restraint you would have to use not to mention this to anyone. Then think of the damage you do by giving in to your weakness. Wouldn't you be proud of yourself if you could keep quiet?

I've often wondered if God allows us to give in to weaknesses so that we can become stronger when we overcome them. In I Corinthians 10:13, Paul says, "No temptation has overtaken you except such as is common to man; but God is faithful, who will not allow you to be tempted beyond what you are able, but with the temptation will also make the way of escape, that you may be able to bear it."

This is an extremely constructive thought to hold in your mind. No weakness you face is beyond your strength. In fact, these weaknesses will, when you overcome them, make you stronger. It stands to reason that it is while you are at your lowest that you have the potential to rise to heights greater than you could ever imagine. I've seen it happen.

A friend once related a story to me about a minister in his community. He did so with the minister's permission, and I'd like to share this story with you.

This minister, a bright, enthusiastic young man, successfully built three churches. He attracted the attention of a group of people who wanted him to come to their community to build a church. He agreed to help them.

After a while, they had 2,200 members and a beautiful building worth nearly $4 million. But the tension and hard work of accomplishing all of this wore on the minister. He couldn't sleep at night, so he went to a doctor, who gave him tranquilizers. Soon, the minister asked for an increased dosage, but the doctor refused. So the minister went to a different doctor, and got stronger drugs. From there, he went into a downward spiral, and his ministry ended.

He sought cures for his dependence, but could not find any that worked. Soon, he was living in a cheap, dirty hotel, begging for money and living on welfare.

Then one day, lying on his hotel-room cot, he suddenly got down by the side of the bed and prayed, "Dear Lord, I'm defeated. I have no power. Such as I am, I ask You to take me and do what You will with me." As he rose from that honest prayer, the thought came to him to go to a certain rehabilitation center. Once in this environment, he felt he had power over his weakness. In a few weeks, he was clean, and he was made chaplain of the center. Three years later, he was elected as the new director.

This minister went from the heights to the depths and then back again to the heights of living. It wasn't easy for him to beat his weakness. It might not be easy for you either, but the power struggle between you and your weakness will be made easier, if you follow this next step.

2. Face Your Weakness. I've been greatly troubled lately by the way so many people are quick to point out the problems our country faces, but few, including politicians, are willing to stand up to these weaknesses and confront them. When we are unwilling to take action to right what's wrong, we're doing a tremendous disservice to our country. And when we are unwilling to stand up to our personal weaknesses, we are doing a disservice to God. He will give us the power to overcome. If we don't take advantage of that power, we are essentially telling God we don't trust Him. When we conquer our personal weaknesses with God's help, we will be armed, and experienced enough, to help conquer the weaknesses of our nation.

How does one confront a weakness? I suggest you learn as much as you can about it. Examine it, chart when you are most vulnerable to it, look at proven methods for diminishing its power over you. Once you understand it, you will be better equipped to defeat it.

I remember a man Norman and I both knew, a man who was defeated and made weak by the blows of life. Here's what happened:

Early one bleak, rainy morning, this man went into a diner for breakfast. Several people were there, but no one was speaking to anyone else. Our miserable friend sat down and hunched over on a stool.

At the other end of the diner was a young mother with a little girl. Suddenly the child broke the sullen silence by saying, "Don't we say grace here, Mommy?"

Behind the counter, the big, burly cook looked at the little girl and said, "Sure we do, honey. Will you say it for us? Then, looking at everyone present, he bellowed, " Bow your heads!"

One by one, the heads went down. The little girl bowed her head and, clasping her hands, said:

"God is great and God is good. And we thank Him for our food. By His hand we all are fed; Give us, Lord, our daily bread."

All of a sudden, the atmosphere changed. People began talking to one another, and the plain, little diner magically turned into a home. All because a little girl gave thanks to God for her food. But more than the diner was transformed. Our friend said, "From that experience, my life changed and gradually I began believing in God, believing in people, and believing in myself."

Our friend got his life together and never again experienced the weakness that led to his depression.

As you work to overcome your weakness, stay alert, and keep studying the weakness. Each time you have a victory, write it down in a journal. As you feel temptation creeping up, go to your journal and relive your victories. Don't be too hard on yourself if you take a few steps backward. Always keep your eyes on your ultimate goal—being free of anything that controls you.

3. Seek Support. In the early years of our marriage, Norman and I shared a common weakness. We both had strong convictions on almost every subject, and sometimes we disagreed. Our problem was to carry on a convincing discussion with one another and always be in control.

We learned how to do this, and became very supportive of each other. We turned what could have been a difficult weakness into a strong understanding relationship.

Whenever one is overwhelmed by a weakness, he should seek every legitimate avenue of help available. In conjunction with seeking earthly support, one should always turn to God. If the two forces—earthly support and heavenly support—are combined, the power to overcome is tremendous. I think this is one of the reasons Alcoholics Anonymous is so successful. Participants are told to surrender themselves to the Higher Power—to God.

Norman loved to tell the story about the time he was invited to a middle-of-the-night prayer meeting. At first, he didn't want to attend, because of the hour and his schedule. Thankfully, he succumbed, and it turned out to be one of the most delightful experiences of his life. Here's what he said about the meeting:

"The house was full of people sitting on the floor, on the stairs, even on the grand piano. People were everywhere, and all were singing old hymns—'Just As I Am,' 'Amazing Grace,' and other familiar hymns. Then they prayed, holding hands as they did so. It was like an electric current flowing throughout the room. Finally, a man rose and walked across the floor with a slight limp. 'I was told I'd never walk again,' he said. When I asked him how come he was walking, he said, 'Jesus did it.'

"A beautiful woman came forward and told how she had been a drug addict, living on the streets of Chicago. She found herself, gained strength over her weakness, and kicked her habit. When I asked her how she did it, she replied, 'Jesus did it.'

"Then a couple stood up, arm in arm. 'You have no idea how we used to fight,' they said. 'We cursed and swore at each other. We hated each other. But now we live happily in love and peace.' When I asked how they did it, I already knew the answer before they spoke: 'Jesus did it,' they said."

I know Norman was touched by this incredible showing of Jesus' power. Let yourself be open to what He can do for you. Honestly tell Jesus what you need done in your life. Then surrender yourself to Him. If you can do this, your weakness will be overpowered.

The longer we dwell on our misfortunes, the greater is their power to harm us.

—Voltaire

CHAPTER 8

Renew Your Health

I shall yet praise him, who is the help of my countenance. —*Psalm 42*

WE'RE living in an age when people are becoming increasingly aware of health issues. National health care proposals are debated by politicians, each fighting for his version. Health care costs have skyrocketed, and the quality of care under a nationalized system is being questioned. The public is justifiably concerned about the direction of health care in America. Out of all this confusion has come a great blessing to the American public: We're learning to be even more aware of, and responsible for, our health.

We already know to cut the fat from our diets, lower our cholesterol, and exercise. Along with these preventive measures, here are three other practical things we can do to renew or maintain our health:

1. Affirm Life. Dr. Sara Jordan, co-founder of the Lahey Clinic in Boston and one of the greatest medical geniuses of the past century, said, "The simple cure for many states of disability is to give your mind a good shampoo every day." Sound too simple to be true? I disagree. A Wisconsin doctor named Schindler used to say that many of his patients were sick because they had what he called the CDTs—cares, difficulties, and troubles. Dr. Schindler said that these problems could not be healed by medicine. What he prescribed for them was this: "Lift the mind for ten minutes every day into the area of pure joy."

Norman often gave the following advice to people under a doctor's care who came to him with complaints of ill health:

Each day, systematically empty your mind of all the mean thoughts, the jealous thoughts, the weak thoughts, all the evil thoughts. Then fill your mind full of good thoughts. Take them right out of the Bible and into your mind. The Bible's thoughts are so powerful that they force out the negative, diseased thoughts. Do this, and you will be following the first way to have good health.

Start each day with this declaration: "God breathed into me the breath of life. This is His life in me. I am God's child. He made me in His own image. He created me; He re-creates me. I shall live with power until, in His judgment, my life here is over; then He will take me to Himself." This is affirmation of life!

Norman and I had a friend who affirmed God's healing power once a day. Although some might think his technique a little unorthodox, he enjoyed good health during his entire 93 years on earth.

Lawrence Townsend was our friend's name. He was a man of many accomplishments. Along with being U.S. ambassador to Austria, he was an expert cabinetmaker who could make a joint so perfectly you could hardly see it.

After visiting Lawrence at his Florida house, Norman told me about our friend's unusual technique for affirming health. In the back of his house, Lawrence had a little enclosure with high wooden walls, but no roof. He would go in there every day, disrobe, and stand in the sunshine or in the rain, whichever it might be. There he would stand lithe and brown as a Native American—at the age of ninety. He would affirm that the healing power of God was flowing through his body, mind, and soul.

Well, you might say he was eccentric, but he lived a good, long life. Norman was tempted to try Lawrence's technique, but was afraid of what the neighbors might think!

You don't have to disrobe in order to make this work for you. Just sit outside, with your face tilted toward the sky and your eyes closed. Then, for a few minutes, affirm that God is breathing good health and a renewed spirit into your body.

2. Keep Your Thoughts Constructive. Some months ago, one of the editors at Peale Center was diagnosed as having leukemia. As long as I've known her, nearly 20 years, she's been a vibrant, healthy, active woman. When we learned of her disease, we were all taken by surprise. But I have a strong faith that she's going to beat this illness, because she's one of the most constructive thinkers I've ever met. She's missed very few work days because of her illness. She's upbeat, optimistic, and busy. How is she maintaining her positive spirit? By doing everything she loves to do. When she's not at Peale Center, she's home quilting, sewing, cooking, gardening, and re-building, along with her husband, their dream house. I'm sure there are times when she worries. That's only natural. But she doesn't dwell on her condition. She's getting on with her life, planning her next quilt, next spring's garden, the color scheme for her new bath-room. She's keeping her thoughts constructive by staying active, praying, and surrounding herself with the people and projects she loves.

You, too, can keep your thoughts constructive when faced with an illness. To do so, you must get rid of your dark, destructive thoughts by turning to the great Physician. He can remove them, if you want them banished.

USA TODAY reports that a recent medical study showed that a highly pessimistic outlook shortens the lifespan of people with re-curring cancer. "It's important not to give up," said the doctor who did this study, Richard Schultz of the University of Pittsburgh. He said that some studies have shown that pessimism can impair one's immune functions, making it harder to fight sickness.

This is one of many studies that prove the power of a positive outlook. And it's not just blind faith, either. Positive thinking is about having a true faith in God, and therefore, in yourself, a true faith in God's ability to heal, and the part you can play in that healing. Posi-tive thinking is about knowing that faith can get you through any-thing.

There is a significant passage in the 42nd Psalm. Because of his physical disability and his inner conflict, the writer of that Psalm was having a great deal of trouble with himself. But again and again, he says: "I shall yet praise him, who is the help of my countenance." He didn't let his many problems drag him down. Instead, he affirmed God and, in so doing, thought constructively.

Casting out the shadows that lurk in our minds requires courage. Never affirm any weakness in yourself. Be humbly conscious of what you are, but never depreciate yourself, as some people do, regarding it as humility. Form and hold mental images of yourself as healthy. Then get on with your life. Plan for your future. See yourself actively healthy, completing a project, holding your grandchildren, vacationing with a loved one. Use whatever images give you the most joy—the most peaceful and relaxed feelings.

3. Develop Calmness. Perhaps the greatest threat to your health is the tyranny of uncontrolled stress and tension. To counteract stress, you need peace, relaxation, silence. Matching stress with calmness will keep your mind and body healthy. One way to accomplish this is to begin and end each day calmly. The importance of this was pointed out to Norman and me by a friend who is a dynamo of driving energy. His daily schedule is packed. Despite his many responsibilities and activities, he handles everything with quiet and impressive power. When asked how he stayed so peaceful under pressure, our friend said, "I have learned how to begin and end each day calmly. If you begin calmly and end calmly, everything that lies between comes under the influence of controlled, dynamic, calm power."

To achieve calmness at the start and end of each day, spend 15 minutes of quiet time each morning and evening, meditating on God's greatness and praying to Him. When my nerves are frazzled and tension is getting the better of me, nothing calms me down better than a good heart-to-heart talk with God. Prayer is vital to maintaining and renewing your health.

Over the years, I have met many physicians who treat their patients with prayer as well as medicine. There were numerous times that doctors called Norman in to pray with them at the bedside of a patient. I remember one specific incident that points out prayer's incredible power.

Norman was awakened one night by a phone call from a doctor. "I am with a patient that you know," he said. "She is very ill." Then he told Norman that she wasn't responding to the treatments he was giving her. "While treating her medically," he said, "I have also been seeking help and guidance in prayer. I feel guided to ask you to come and join me in applying faith to this critical situation."

Norman went, and found the patient in a coma. "Let's try to reach her at a deep level of consciousness and stimulate in her the desire to live," the doctor suggested. "This, together with the medical steps I've taken, may perhaps bring healing." The doctor sat on one side of the bed, Norman on the other.

A nurse stood at the foot of the patient's bed. They prayed silently, then aloud. Then something extraordinary happened. The doctor quoted several Scripture passages. Norman did the same.

To their astonishment, both realized they were quoting, almost verbatim, passages that they did not know that well.

This continued for a few hours. Daylight began shining in the room when suddenly the patient stirred, looked at the two men, and smiled faintly.

"She has come out of the coma," said the doctor after examining her. "All of her vital signs are good. God has been here tonight."

Prayer can renew, or help you maintain, your health. I'm a firm believer in specific prayer. When I found out that my associate at Peale Center was diagnosed with leukemia, the first thing I did was ask her what exactly was going on inside of her body. When she told me that her white blood cell count was too high, I told her that I'd pray for, and visualize, it coming down into normal range. Whenever possible, be specific in your prayers.

Don't be afraid to let God know what you want, but remember that He has His reasons for the twists and turns our lives take. As you put the matter of your health in God's hands, let Him know that you are open to accepting His will. Also affirm your own health by thanking God for your wellness. And, remember to pray as mightily as you can for other people who are ill or suffering.

It is my hope that you enjoy many, many years of good health. Take care of yourself. God has important work for you to do!

A man too busy to take care of his health is like a mechanic too busy to take care of his tools.

—Spanish proverb

CHAPTER 9

Break Your Bad Habits Forever!

Let the weak say, I am strong.

—Joel 3:10

"GOOD MORNING," said the smiling young woman as she exuberantly entered the elevator. After greeting her in the same manner, I told her that she seemed to be exceptionally happy.

"Oh," she said, "yes, I guess so, but I don't know. I've got an awful lot of worrying to do today. It's a habit of mine. I worry every day." With that comment, the elevator door opened and the young woman left, quickly disappearing down the hall.

As the elevator continued on, I wondered if I should return to the floor where the young woman had exited. If I tracked her down, perhaps I could help her get over this unhealthy habit. Unfortunately, circumstances wouldn't allow me to do this, for I was with someone else and we were pressed for time.

But the image of that young woman carrying the burden of a worry habit has stayed with me since that day. So it is for you and her and for all of us that I write this, for no one should be a slave to any habit. Here are four ways you can break free from destructive habits, no matter how strong a hold they have on you.

1. Understand Your Habit. Bad habits creep up on us and often overcome our better senses. Who among us truly believes that worry accomplishes anything? Yet some of us allow this troubling habit to continue operating in our lives. And even though we know that negative thinking is not productive, we give this irksome habit the power to dominate us. Any habit that has the potential to ruin your life should be eradicated, and you can do it! How do I know this? I've seen people whose bad habits knocked them lower than you and I can ever imagine being—people who sprang back and walked away from potentially destroying their lives. One of the key elements that enabled these people to break bad habits was their ability to understand their habits.

A habit is an acquired tendency that becomes strong from mindless repetition. The good news is that habits can be broken by breaking the chain of repetition. And we can do it by putting our faith and our minds to work. Look at your habit closely. What sets it off? For example, if your bad habit is smoking, does stress make you reach for a cigarette? If worry is the habit you need to break, what situations trigger your worry? Norman had the habit of overeating when he was nervous or tense. When he suddenly began gaining weight, he became even more tense. For a while, he was trapped by this unhealthy habit. But once he realized that he was reaching for food to soothe himself, he was able to break the chain of repetition.

Stress seems to be the main trigger that sets off many of our unhealthy habits. After a nerve-racking day at work, you might think to yourself, *A few cocktails will help me unwind.* But there are going to be other nerve-wracking days. Will a few drinks to ease stress turn into an every night occurrence?

Logically, we all know that stress is not going to be controlled by food, worry, or any other bad habit. Bad habits are just going to add more stress to our lives, so it's vital to work on this next habit-breaking step.

2. Minimize Stress. We have to be realistic. We are all going to experience stressful situations. That's a part of life. What we can do, though, is to minimize the stress in our lives. There are two ways to do this easily: first, learn to relax and second, dispose of the worthless thoughts in your mind.

To rid yourself of these worthless thoughts, try letting go of negative emotions such as hate, anger, envy, or feelings of guilt. A conscience laden with bad feelings will cause you more stress than any outside factor possibly could.

Let me tell you about a man whose guilt nurtured his obsessive habit.

This man would always, after turning off the bathroom faucet, go back to the sink three times to make sure the water was off. He would also try the door three times to make sure it was locked. He worried that unless he performed these little rituals, a terrible thing would happen. And if, for some reason, he didn't check the faucet and door three times, he spent his entire day in turmoil.

The tension this man lived under was self-inflicted. He eventually sought counseling, for he knew these habits, though seemingly harmless, were destroying his mental state. As it turned out, he was subconsciously punishing himself through his obsessive habits, for some past transgressions. He eventually confessed his sins to God, sought His forgiveness, and believed that God did indeed forgive him. A new-found peacefulness entered his life and, over time, he was able to break his habit.

As you are trying to break your habit, it is essential for you to reduce the tension in your life. The key elements here are: relaxation, confession, and the ability to receive God's forgiveness.

3. Will Yourself To Beat the Habit. Once you understand your habit and reduce the amount of stress in your life, you are ready to work on your willpower. Let this statement from the Old Testament become your motto as you work to break your habit: . . . "Let the weak say, I am strong" (Joel 3:10).

Believe you are strong, stronger than any habit that has taken hold of you. If you do this, you will become so. Here, from one of Norman's sermons, are some words of encouragement for you to keep in mind:

How do you reach goals? By the application of a twin principle: to will and to believe. Willpower is the process by which you bring out of yourself an enormous force. Believing is the process by which you bring out of yourself the power of God. So to will means to bring out your personal power; to believe means to bring out God's power.

What do you want to accomplish? Will it! There is a powerful spiritual and psychological force given to people who exercise willpower. They achieve their goals despite all kinds of odds.

If you feel your willpower is soft, exercise it. Think of your will-power as a flabby muscle that has to be strengthened. As with any muscle, repeated use will toughen it up. You can make your will-power stronger by first exercising it on smaller matters.

Start by doing things you consider difficult. For instance, if you are uncomfortable around strangers, attend an event where you won't know anyone. Force yourself to speak with people. Also, practice disciplining yourself a few times each day. Make yourself take a walk. Make yourself get up five minutes earlier each morning. Make yourself drive on a road you usually avoid. Think of ways to challenge your will and set at least two goals a day for yourself.

This process will strengthen your willpower and ready you for this final habit-breaking step.

4. Ask for Help. Some people act as if bad habits are a disgrace, something to be concealed at all costs. Others might grimly say to themselves, "This is my problem. I'll work it out myself." Such attitudes are mistakes, for we are strengthened when we seek help.

From whom should you seek help? You can get tremendous habit-breaking support from anyone who has overcome your habit. Support groups exist for those who wish to quit smoking, drinking, overeating, and gambling. Check your local newspaper or library for the names of organizations that can meet your needs.

Doctors, ministers, and professional counselors can also greatly aid you in your habit-breaking quest. Even a sympathetic friend or loved one can help by listening or offering encouragement. Sharing your struggle with others will ease your strain. Plus, once you tell someone you want to break a habit, you've made an important commitment to at least try.

Don't forget to also ask Jesus for His help, for it is through Him that you will derive your greatest aid. Time after time, I've heard from people who, seeing no way out of their self-destructive habits, turned to Jesus. All of these people experienced a miraculous turnaround. Here's an excerpt from a letter we received from one such person:

> I suffered a crushing blow. I lost a career of twenty-seven years, a wife, and three beautiful children. I almost killed

myself by abusing cigarettes, food, alcohol, and drugs. Spiritually dead, I cried out to Jesus, and He answered my cry. I gave my life to Jesus as I had made a mess of it and just couldn't handle it anymore.

Today, I am a new man with a new life. I have started a second career and I have remarried. My wife is my most precious gift from the Lord. I teach a Bible study in my home, jog, and attend church regularly.

I am well and happy. I have more problems than you could shake a stick at, but I am God's son. I laugh and work and play in His care and His wonderful world. All is not perfect, but now I have Jesus to get me through.

This man was a slave to habits that eventually would have killed him, but he broke free. And what joy radiates from his words. Everything in his life might not be perfect, but he's not letting those troubles weaken his resistance. With Jesus' help, he has built up a wall between himself and his old habits. You can, too! Never hesitate to ask Jesus for His help.

When you turn to Jesus, ask Him to strengthen you with a "never-give-up" attitude. In this way, if you at first fail at your habit-breaking attempt, you'll feel reassured that you will try again. Also, affirm the following while speaking to Jesus:

Thank you, dear Lord, for now You are increasing my faith, strengthening my resolve, renewing my enthusiasm, helping me to hang in there, and fight the good fight.

Bad habits are meant to be broken and can stay broken—forever. They are a challenge for us that we should never shy away from. Our victories over bad habits make us stronger and more confident. So look forward to the battle, for the reward is sweet.

Good habits are as easy to form as bad ones.

—Tim Carver

CHAPTER 10

How To Make Each Day Productive

He who sows sparingly will also reap sparingly, and he who sows bountifully will also reap bountifully.

—II Corinthians 9:6

THIS morning, my mind raced as I thought of all the things I have to do today. I'm used to busy days, and I enjoy them, But this morning, I felt overwhelmed by the responsibilities facing me. As I rushed through the house, getting ready to go to the office, I glanced at a framed photograph of Norman. All of a sudden, I felt less agitated, remembering what a calming influence Norman always had on me. Then, I went into the study to pray. I immediately felt my mind clearing, my energy level rising, and God's peaceful strength. I was ready to make my day a productive one.

Norman used to comment about the "things-to-do" notes I make for myself, and my need to squeeze as much as possible into each day. But he appreciated this ability, which I'd like to try to pass on to you. Here's how you can do what needs to be done each day.

1. Energize Yourself. Without energy, we cannot accomplish anything. Of course, you know that a good night's sleep is of vital importance. But there is another re-energizing method available to you: Spend at least ten minutes each morning in prayer and meditation. During these ten-minute periods, you are waiting on God, getting closer and closer to Him. And God is the source of our renewed strength, mind, and spirit.

Norman often quoted Isaiah 40:31: "They that wait upon the Lord shall renew their strength; they shall mount up with wings as eagles; they shall run, and not be weary; they shall walk, and not faint." Here is how he interpreted this verse:

These words significantly teach a rare form of climax. One rises up like an eagle in a tremendous upthrusting burst of energy. But the climax is to keep going when the going is tough, and not faint, which is another way of saying, "Don't give up." You get the energy for the long difficult trek, for the hard-going times.

Norman also suggested that we personalize this Biblical formula for energy by using this creative affirmation: "I am waiting on the Lord. Therefore I am renewing my strength. I am mounting up with wings like an eagle. I can run and not grow tired. I can walk when the walking is not easy. And I shall never have to stop going. I thank God for this miracle of undiminished energy."

The fact that energy is renewed simply through prayer and meditation has been made evident to me many times. So, before you begin your day's work, take ten minutes to energize yourself. Then, if you find your energy waning later in the day, take another ten minutes to boost yourself up.

I've also learned that a cluttered mind depletes energy and causes disorganization. To avoid confused thinking that leads to a nonproductive day, I make notes of things as they pass through my mind. For instance, if I want to mention an article idea to one of our editors, I'll jot down my thought and put it in a pile of such notes that I will later sift through. When I go through my notes, I put them in order of importance. We'll talk about setting priorities later. For now, let's go on to another important factor in making each day productive.

2. Get, and Stay, Enthused. The president of a large company once said: "If you have two people of fairly equal ability, but the less able person has enthusiasm, he will go farther than the other person, because there is a self-releasing power about enthusiasm that tends to focus the entire force of the individual. Enthusiasm, like an infection, carries all before it."

I agree with this. A person with enthusiasm always wants to learn, to accomplish, to do his or her best. Harvey Mackay, in his best-selling book *Sharkproof,* writes of a young man who, with little experience and a high school education, landed a $75,000-a-year job. When he asked why he was hired over more experienced people, he was told it was because of his enthusiasm and freshness. His employer obviously recognized the value of an enthusiastic employee.

Whether your work is housework, homework, paid employment or volunteer duties, you'll find that your productivity rises as your enthusiasm rises. I've found that once I start working on a project, I can maintain my enthusiasm for it by looking for the interesting aspects of what I'm doing. Everything we do is of interest if we use our imaginations. For instance, let's say you work in an automobile factory, and you perform the same tasks each day. Try looking past the job. Think about how this car you helped assemble will run for years, taking children to soccer games, carrying an elderly person to church, enabling a teen-ager to be driven off to college. We should see that the end results of all our work are positive. We just must take the time, and use our imaginations, to look that far ahead.

You can plow right through your daily tasks, if you change the way you look at them. When you apply enthusiasm to a job, the job becomes alive with exciting new possibilities. The following story illustrates this point.

We knew a dull life-insurance agent who lived hand-to-mouth. His sales record was poor, and he constantly told his wife what a mistake he made getting into the insurance business. His wife was a wise woman. She got her husband to pray, and encouraged him to believe in himself. One morning before he started out of the house, he prayed: "Lord, fill me with enthusiasm for life insurance." That may sound like a strange prayer, but it was his livelihood. Then he added: "Lord, fill me with enthusiasm for what I can do for people by selling them life insurance."

That day, he sold two policies. Then he went on to become one of the company's most successful salespeople. "I discovered," he told us, "that if an ordinary man believes enthusiastically in the things he is doing, he can do them in an extraordinary manner."

To maintain your enthusiasm throughout the day, do these two things: First, repeat to yourself the following: "This job is really challenging. Thank you, God, for this opportunity to prove myself." Then, every few hours, take five minutes to review the tasks you have completed. Once you look at what you've done, you'll feel encouraged and ready to cover more ground.

3. Don't Procrastinate. There's a little bit of the procrastinator in all of us, whether we're putting off washing the dog or dealing with some pesky problem at work. But we all have to inevitably deal with that which we put off. And the more tasks we put off, the more they pile up. This spells disaster, especially for someone easily overwhelmed by a heavy workload.

When I know I have a lot to do, I get up at least one hour earlier than normal. This extra hour makes a big difference in what I accomplish. I go into my office at Peale Center and I'm able to work with little interruption, since there are so few people around.

Another method I suggest for overcoming procrastination is keeping track of what needs to be done. I mentioned that I make notes throughout the day. I take these notes and put them into a list, which I review. Priorities are moved to the top of the list. I consider a priority anything that helps another person. My next priority is to meet all of my deadlines. And so on. Sometimes I find that I do have to put off tasks, because I need to give them more thought. But I always go back to those tasks after a day or two of praying about them.

Determine right now that tomorrow you are going to accomplish something you've been putting off. Then, plan the reward you'll give yourself for completing the job. I think tomorrow I'll finish writing that article I put aside days ago. Then I'll treat myself to that new book I've been wanting to read.

4. If You Need Help, Ask. I'm fortunate. I learned long ago that I cannot do everything by myself. And, I'm not hesitant about asking for help. (Just ask my secretary, Sybil.) This is a lesson that we all must take seriously. If you're a homemaker, ask your husband and children for help in doing some of the household chores. If you're a boss, delegate. If you are in a position where you can't delegate, go to your boss and tell him or her when you need help. If you take on more than you can handle, everything you do will suffer as a result.

Even the simple act of asking God for His help makes an incredible difference in allowing you to get things done. I remember a time in Norman's life when he didn't feel up to all the job pressures that were put upon him.

He and I sat and talked about it while on vacation. My advice to him was to tell the Lord that he couldn't handle all of those problems by himself. I also suggested that he ask God to take over his life, and believe that God loved him and would guide him. Norman did just that. Instantly, an incredible change came over him. "Let's end our vacation and go back to New York at once," he said. "I want to get back on the job!"

"Oh my," I said, "maybe I've gone too far with this." But return we did. And the job problems that haunted him weren't as daunting, because Norman was different. He had turned to God for help.

God is always there to help us, and people are, too. I've found people are glad to help out, as long as you don't take advantage of them and, of course, work hard yourself.

I pray that these suggestions have given you useful ideas on ways you can make each day more productive. I believe we should make the most of every moment God gives us. "He who sows sparingly will also reap sparingly, and he who sows bountifully will also reap bountifully" (II Corinthians 9:6).

Success seems to be largely a matter of hanging on after others have let go.

—William Feather

CHAPTER 11

Forgive Yourself, Forgive Others

. . . Be kind to one another, tenderhearted, forgiving one another, just as God in Christ also has forgiven you. —Ephesians 4:31-32

I STARTED to read the following letter, which began: "I have a serious problem and I need help. I have a very bad grudge against someone I used to think so much of. I have built up a terrible amount of resentment against this person to the point that I cannot sleep at night and have become depressed."

As I read these words, I thought to myself, *How sad that the act of forgiveness is so difficult for so many people.* You see, that letter echoes the same problem I see repeatedly: a wife who can't forgive her husband's infidelity; a daughter who cannot forgive her father's verbal abuse; an employee who cannot forgive an employer, the list goes on and on. Also, on the other side of our personalities, is the inability to forgive ourselves for past transgressions. And when we cannot forgive ourselves and forget our mistakes, we live with dark clouds that keep us from enjoying the good things in life. Ultimately, this failure on our part can also make us ill—mentally, spiritually, and physically.

Isn't it time for each of us to examine seriously those people we consider unforgivable, so that we can begin healing ourselves and our relationship? Here is what you can do:

1. Simply Determine To Forgive. "Let all bitterness, wrath, anger, clamor, and evil speaking be put away from you, with all malice. And be kind to one another, tenderhearted, forgiving one another, just as God in Christ also has forgiven you" (Ephesians 4:31-32). This simple, direct blueprint should become your mantra as you set your mind to the act of forgiveness.

The ability to feel sincere forgiveness toward another is not easy, and the longer you hold onto a resentment, the harder it is to eradicate that ugly feeling. Soon, the resentment becomes habit. To break away, you have to decide that, no matter what, you will be forgiving toward anyone who has hurt you.

As part of your determination, take concrete steps. First, make a list of those people you need to forgive. If you need to forgive yourself, include your own name. Then, beside each name, write down how you've been hurt by that person. Next, set a date and time for the acts of forgiveness to take place. Be realistic. Don't expect to perform a blanket act of forgiveness by tomorrow at noon. Take seriously the idea that you are going to work to conscientiously forgive each person on your list. Each of these actions may take some time. Finally, beside each name, write down a way for you to communicate your forgiveness to the person involved. You may consider writing a letter, making a phone call, or paying a visit. Whatever you choose, bring God into the process by seeking His wisdom as you write, phone, or visit. He'll guide your words if you turn to Him for help.

When you are ready to begin this healing process, take the next step, if it applies. And from all that I've seen over the years, it more than likely does.

2. Forgive Yourself. There are many of us who have made mistakes, and lived to regret them deeply. As a result, we repeatedly torture ourselves over something that may have happened a long time ago, wishing we could turn the clock back and re-live the moment. These mistakes may be great or small. That fact is inconsequential. What matters is our inability to say, "I forgive myself."

If we cannot honestly do this, it is probably because we haven't truly sought forgiveness. To do so, you must first ask God to forgive you. If you shortcut this step, you'll never truly be able to forgive yourself. And the effect of not doing so could have devastating consequences on your life.

The experience of an acquaintance bears this out. Here's what happened:

Tom, as I will call him to protect his privacy, was, at one

time, a dynamic community and business leader. But he became depressed and indifferent. His wife, concerned over the change in Tom's personality, sought help. She wrote to Norman, asking him to visit Tom. Norman obliged. The first thing he noticed when he saw Tom was that the man (who was relatively young) shuffled when he walked. And he held his arms in the same manner a stroke victim would. Now, Norman knew from speaking with Tom's wife that the physicians could not find any physical reason for Tom's maladies. Yet, his whole demeanor, even his voice, made him appear as though he were an invalid.

After talking with Norman for a while, Tom admitted to not caring about anyone or anything. "The life has been knocked out of me," he said. Then, Norman surprised Tom with his direct approach. "Tom," he said, "have you talked to anyone about all that stuff you are holding in your mind? Your doctor says there is nothing wrong with you, so the inference is that there may be a heavy burden on your mind, or perhaps even on your soul.

"If you will unload this burden, and give it to Jesus Christ, He will clean out your mind, forgive you, and you can be your old self again. So, what do you say we get on with it?"

Tom look at Norman piteously. "How do you know so much about me? Who told you?"

"No one told me," Norman said. "I know no facts about you, but I do know that anyone afflicted as you are must be in deep soul trouble."

Norman's talk caused the floodgates to open. Suddenly, Tom talked with great intensity about the many shameful things he had done. When Tom was through, Norman asked him if he was sincerely sorry for his wrongdoings. He said that he was. Then Norman guided him to seek God's forgiveness, which he did.

Afterward, they sat quietly. Then something interesting happened. Slowly, Tom got to his feet and began to stretch. In a strong, exultant voice, he exclaimed, "My, but I feel good!"

And as he walked Norman to the door, his step was livelier. His whole being projected vigor and happiness. The tremendous weight of guilt Tom carried had been lifted through God's grace.

So, if you need to forgive yourself, first seek God's forgiveness. Confess your sins, ask for God's forgiveness, and then thank Him for granting it. There's also a second step to this process. If you need to forgive yourself, it's possible that you have wronged someone. You must make amends.

In his book *Seventy Times Seven,* Johann Christoph Arnold recounts the story of a Vietnam veteran who was haunted by feelings of guilt. John Plummer was a helicopter pilot who organized a napalm raid on a small village. It happened that during this raid, a photographer took a picture of a nine-year-old Vietnamese girl, standing naked and crying, her body burned and arms outstretched. The picture received worldwide attention. It also received Plummer's attention and caused him a great deal of torment. He had done everything he could to make sure the village was cleared before the bombing began, but still he tortured himself over what had happened to that child. As Arnold puts it, Plummer "turned in on himself, his marriage failed, and he began to drink."

Then, according to the author, an incredible thing happened in 1996. Plummer saw the photographed girl, Phan Thi Kim Phuc, at the Vietnam Veterans Memorial in Washington, DC.

Kim was there to lay a wreath of peace. Plummer was there to fight the demons of his past. Kim and Plummer met. He told her that he was responsible for the bombing of her village and he sought her forgiveness. "Kim saw my grief, my pain, my sorrow," he later said. "She held out her arms to me and embraced me. All I could say was 'I'm sorry, I'm sorry'—over and over again. And at the same time, she was saying, 'It's all right, I forgive you.'"

This incredible story doesn't end there. In the years that have followed their meeting, Kim and Plummer became close friends, and Plummer's life was healed. Seeking Kim's forgiveness freed him to forgive himself. This same wonderful blessing can occur in your life. Seek forgiveness and it shall be yours.

3. Forgive Others. Keep this verse in mind: ". . . Be kind to one another, tenderhearted, forgiving one another, just as God in Christ also has forgiven you" (Ephesians 4:31-32). You are forgiven whenever you seek forgiveness. This is a tremendous gift that God gives to you. Why, then, would you hold back forgiveness toward others? This is a gift that is to be shared. We are instructed "to be kind and tenderhearted" toward one another—no matter what happens.

In Father Brian Cavanaugh's book *Sower's Seeds Aplenty,* I read a touching story about forgiveness written by Doris Donnelly. I'd like to retell it to you.

A mother and her two young sons were riding in their car. The mother, unhappy over her husband's recent abandonment of the family, was feeling extremely distraught. Suddenly, in a fit of anger, she turned and slapped her seven-year-old son in the face. "I never wanted you," she screamed. "The only reason I had you was to keep your father. But then he left anyway. I hate you!"

For 23 years, he relived that memory, always recalling the fact that his mother "hated him and did not want him." The fact that his mother constantly found fault with him reinforced this memory. But remarkably, when he grew into adulthood, he was able to do something that many of us fail to do.

Here are his words: "Recently, I put myself in my mother's shoes. Here she was, a high-school graduate with no skills, no job, no money, and a family to support. I realized how lonely and depressed she must have felt. I thought of her anger and pain. And I thought of how much I reminded her of the failure of her young hopes. So one day, I decided to visit her and talk to her. I told her that I understood her feelings and that I loved her just the same. She broke down and we wept in each other's arms for what seemed to be hours. It was the beginning of a new life for me, for her—for both of us."

This young man, who could have been beaten down by the way his mother treated him, rose above it with a grace we should all aspire to. He could have lived a failed, miserable life, blaming it all on his terrible childhood. Instead, he did the Christian thing. He put himself in her shoes, walked, and forgave.

Here, now, are some specific suggestions on forgiving others. They come from Norman's book *How To Make Positive Imaging Work for You:*

• Resist the temptation to be judgmental. Remember, only God knows all the circumstances. Leave the judging to Him.

• Learn to be compassionate. Put yourself in the other person's shoes, ask yourself whether the fault is entirely the other person's or whether you are partially responsible for the situation.

• Image the whole problem in terms of reconciliation. Visualize the broken relationship healed. See yourself freed of the poisons of resentment and anger.

• Pray for the person who has offended you. If this is difficult (and it will be), pray for God's grace to come into your heart to give you the strength to do it. Remind yourself that the act of forgiveness will benefit you.

• End with the Lord's Prayer. Give special thought and emphasis to the part that asks God to forgive us our debts as we forgive our debtors.

There are two marks of a holy person: giving and forgiving. —Anonymous

CHAPTER 12

How To Make Right Decisions

Thou shalt guide me with thy counsel, and afterward receive me to glory.

—Psalm 73:24

L IFE is a series of choices and the quality of our lives depends upon the decisions we make, big and small. When we take charge and make right decisions, happiness and fulfillment await us. When we let life happen to us because we don't know which way to turn, we are left wondering what could have been. For your happiness, it is necessary for you to take charge of your life and learn how to make the right decisions.

For example, here is the story of Chicago's Karla Osantowski.

Pregnant at 16, Karla dropped out of school. A few years later, she found herself in an abusive marriage. At 22, she decided she could no longer stand the abuse. Scared and penniless, but determined, she and her two young daughters left their home. They moved into a housing project, and Karla began receiving public assistance.

It was at this low point that she took charge of her life and her next set of decisions totally changed everything. She saw that the only way to get off welfare and out of the projects was through education. So she earned her high-school equivalency certificate, and this enabled her to get a job. While working full time, she signed up for evening classes. Eventually, Karla graduated from Loyola University with a degree in criminal justice.

She assumed she would find a spot in the Chicago police department, but there were no vacancies. So another decision waited. She returned to school and acquired a degree in law.

Karla Osantowski became a prosecutor and volunteered to help victims of domestic violence. Her abilities were noticed and, in time, she was offered the job as the Chicago Heights police chief. In this position, she has won the admiration and respect of her co-workers and the people she serves. She's also fulfilled a dream that for many may have seemed unattainable: an uneducated, abused, poor young mother pulled herself out of a black hole and is now thriving.

The mistakes Karla made early in life gave her the ability to realize the importance of taking charge of one's own life and making decisions. "People say you have to play the hand that's dealt you, but I don't believe that for a minute," she said. "If you don't like the hand, reshuffle the deck."

Here are three ways you can reshuffle the deck and begin to make right decisions.

1. Let Rightness Lead You. You can never arrive at a wise decision unless you base it on ethical rightness. To get right answers, you have to be right.

So many people have trouble with their decisions because they make them knowing there was wrongness in them. Most of us know when something is wrong and when it is right. Some may fool themselves into thinking that they don't know or that there is sometimes a gray area between right and wrong. I strongly deny that. Right is right. And wrong is wrong.

When you permit an unethical factor to invade your decisions, the results will be unfortunate. Your decision won't be soundly based and it won't hold up.

A friend of Norman's found this to be true when he faced a tough decision.

Harold, a successful commercial artist, often received jobs that required him to create art that was sexually provocative. The going rate for his off-colored art was higher than his pay for decent art, he told Norman.

Then Harold started going to church, and he committed

himself to Jesus Christ. One day, Harold's supervisor assigned him the job of creating a piece of art that went way beyond the bounds of good taste. Now he was up against his first tough decision as a Christian. Harold firmly believed that it would be wrong for him to take on this assignment. His loyalty to Jesus meant that he must now live by a higher ethical standard.

Although his boss admired Harold's honesty and courage, he could no longer employ him. Without a job, but with the loving support of his wife, Harold knew he had done the right thing. As days passed, Harold prayed that he would find another job.

One day, a man from an employment agency called Harold. "There's a big job calling for a top-flight illustrator," he said, "and you've been recommended highly." Later, Harold discovered that the recommendation came from the boss who had fired him.

Harold's decision won him a better, more fulfilling job. And it also won him the admiration of his former employer, who was not used to seeing people stand up for what they believe in.

Whenever you have a tough decision to make, ask God to reduce the error of your thinking and to enhance the rightness. This prayer will help:

Lord, help me to adhere to justice and goodness and honor and rightness, knowing that as I do so, I will make decisions that are solidly based and my life will become increasingly creative and satisfying and pleasing to You. For this I give You thanks, through Jesus Christ our Lord. Amen.

After you have removed those gray areas from your thinking, you will find yourself ready for this next step.

2. Clear Your Mind. Good decisions cannot be made when one's mind is full of confusion or when the mind is preoccupied by other matters. Good decision-making requires logic and order, which can only take place in a clear, peaceful mind.

The problem is that when many of us are faced with a tough decision, we panic. And panic is a guaranteed mind-clouder. In order to make right decisions, you need to quiet your mind. The following story illustrates the value of this technique:

A businessman I knew was faced with a tremendous decision. He struggled with it day and night. He couldn't sleep and became extremely tense and irritable. The more he wrestled with the decision, the more complex it seemed.

Then, pacing in his office one day, he happened to pause in front of his mother's picture. She had been a good, simple woman whom he loved and admired. As he looked at his mother's photo, he recalled wise advice she had given him many times. "Let's just let the problem rest a while and think about God."

His mother's words seemed like a direct message to him. He sat down at his desk, removed all of the papers strewn about it, and consciously said to himself, "I will turn away from this problem for a while." From one of his drawers, he pulled out a Bible. He then settled back in his chair and started reading the Book of Psalms. He did this for one hour. Finally, he closed the Bible and sat quite still, thinking about nothing but God.

Afterward, a feeling of calm pervaded his thoughts. His mind grew quiet and relaxed. Refreshed, he returned to work. While there, he thought of a business acquaintance down the street whom he suddenly had the urge to see. Acting upon this impulse, he visited with the man. And, during the course of their conversation, my friend had a flash of insight, which led him to make a decision. Subsequent events proved that the decision he arrived upon, after clearing his mind, was indeed the correct one.

Here are some simple ways you can clear your mind before making a difficult decision: First, go into a quiet place, free of any distractions. Relax your mind and body by getting into a comfortable position and closing your eyes. Next, repeat three times the following text from Psalm 73:24: "Thou shalt guide me with thy counsel, and afterward receive me to glory." This text will remind you that you have access to God's advice. Finally, deliberately conceive of God's advice as passing into your mind and be assured that in due time you will know what that advice is.

3. Be Willing To Accept God's Decision. Confide in God when you must reach a decision. Ask for His guidance. Then be willing to accept the answer He gives you. This sounds easy enough but there are times when what we want isn't what God wants for us.

The main thing to keep in mind is that God's wisdom is beyond our understanding, so we must trust His guidance—even if it sometimes defies our emotions or logic. For example, put yourself in the following true-life situation:

A young woman we knew had been bequeathed a substantial fortune by her father. But the property was tangled in a legal mess and was in litigation. The young lady did not have the funds to fight the litigation, but was rescued when a friend, who was a lawyer, decided to assist her.

After a lengthy trial, a verdict was reached against the young woman. As they walked away from the courthouse, the dejected lawyer turned to his friend and asked her how she felt. He was surprised when she answered that she felt perfectly fine. "Don't you realize what has happened?" he asked her. "You are penniless. You have lost everything!"

Calmly, she answered him. "All through the trial, I prayed that God's will be done. I couldn't pray for victory unless God wanted it so, and I have prayed that the trial turn out as God wanted it to be. I accept this and feel only peace in my heart." Her friend looked at her in amazement. She looked incredibly serene.

Months later, this woman had a dream that God wanted her to take the case to a higher court, so she did. Her friend reopened the case and was able to get a verdict in the woman's favor. As it turned out, she reaped substantially more benefits than she would have had if she had won the first case.

This incident emphasizes how important it is to sincerely pray

151

that God's will be done. The young lady I just told you about wanted nothing for herself unless God willed it so.

As you face decisions, keep these final few points in mind: Never hurry your decision. Weigh your problem carefully. After prayerful consideration and upon reaching your decision, thank God for giving you the right answer. Also, thank Him for giving you an answer that is spiritually correct. Finally, having reached your decision, trust it wholeheartedly. Do not look back and rehash the whole thing. If you have sought God's counsel and prayed earnestly, your answer will come up as a clear, bright light burning in your mind. You can trust it to lead you through the darkness. God will see you through.

God never made a promise that was too good to be true.
—D. L. Moody

CHAPTER 13

Enjoy the Benefits of Giving

Bring ye all tithes into the storehouses . . .

—Malachi 3:10

ARE YOU overwhelmed, as many are, with thoughts of giving? December is usually a month of pressure, because many of us try to squeeze a year's worth of gift giving into one month. Besides family and friends, there's the mail carrier, the newspaper carrier, the garbage hauler, the physician who was especially kind, the neighbor who watched your house while you were out of town—any number of people whose service and kindness you appreciate.

Why limit your giving to a few weeks? There are many opportunities to give during the year, so there is no reason to squeeze our generosity into such a short time frame. Happiness comes from giving. Wouldn't it be wonderful to keep that feeling going?

Here's how you can incorporate giving into your everyday lifestyle:

1. Gift Your Faith. You may be a bit timid about gifting your faith, fearing that your recipient may not be receptive. But the gift of faith is the most meaningful gift in the world, and you can give it to anyone, anytime. Even if your gift of faith is presented just as a small seed, it has the potential to grow and become the gift of a lifetime.

Here are several suggestions to help guide you:

If you enjoy the company of children, volunteer to read Bible stories to a Sunday school class. Follow your reading with a fun activity—one that relates to the story you've just read.

If you're at ease with older people, give your faith to an elder by visiting a nursing home. Ask the director for the names of one or two residents who do not receive regular visitors. Introduce yourself to one of them. At the end of your visit, offer to pray with your new friend. A few days after your visit, send the resident a note and include an inspiring Bible verse in your closing. As you are able, keep the relationship going through visits, notes, and phone calls.

You can also give the gift of your faith by doing something as simple as having personal stationery printed with a Bible verse as a heading. Choose a verse that will touch others as well as one that means a great deal to you.

One car-wash owner in our area has decided to gift his faith to the community and his customers in a unique way. Every week, in plastic letters, he places a different Scripture verse on his business sign. Since the business is located on a busy road, many people are touched by his gift of faith each day.

Will your gift of faith really make a difference in another person's life? Here is an example of the life-changing power this gift can have.

One evening, in Brooklyn, N.Y., a bunch of rough teen-aged boys were sitting around a table. There was tension in the air as the leader spoke. He directed his anger and words at a fellow member, Lou, who had just informed the others that he wanted out of the gang. He was tired of stealing and mugging.

But the leader would not accept the resignation. When Lou wouldn't budge on his decision, the leader commanded the others to tie him up. The members carried Lou to a car and then drove him to an abandoned shack in an isolated area. Once inside, they tied Lou to a chair so that he was sitting backward. Then they ripped off his shirt and, one by one, carved their initials into his flesh. That was so Lou wouldn't ever forget them.

The boy woke up in a hospital. The pain was incredible. Each time he moved, he felt as though he was being stabbed in the back. Lou lay in that bed thinking about how much he hated the gang members. He also planned his revenge. "I'll get every one of them, even if it takes my whole life," he told himself.

Then one day, a young black man named Ben came to visit the boy. This man, one of the most valiant Christians Norman and I ever knew, devoted his life to helping troubled young people. Ben, confident in the value of his gift of faith, didn't pull any punches with the ex-gang member. Ben talked about the world, about the upheavals and breakdowns and hatreds in society. He also talked about the glorious role of Jesus in the salvation of mankind. And what Ben had to say fascinated Lou. So much so that, while still lying there in that hospital bed, he accepted Jesus into his life. He also forgave the gang members who had carved him up, and he vowed that he would try to bring Jesus to them, just as Ben had brought Jesus to him.

Ben gave his faith and Lou was re-born. You can make the same type of difference in someone's life with your gift of faith. Take a moment right now to plan a gift of faith. Fill in the following blank: I'll give the gift of my faith by_____.

2. Give Yourself. So many of us are wrapped up in our own lives. We know that there are tremendous needs in the world, but we feel inadequate when it comes to doing anything about them. We need to remember that we can make a difference in the lives of others simply by giving ourselves.

I've always advocated community involvement. You can determine the level of your involvement by the amount of extra time you have. Even if you give yourself to a worthwhile cause for one hour a week, you and those you serve will benefit. Older people make wonderful volunteers, perhaps because they have a level of patience that some younger people are yet to acquire. I read of a group of older women who are having a lot of fun giving the gift of their time.

Good Housekeeping magazine recently ran an article about 17 senior volunteers who call themselves the Golden Gals. These women spend a lot of their spare time caring for the elderly residents of Beth Abraham Health Services in New York City.

According to the article, one of the volunteers, Mary Allison, is, at 83, one of the younger volunteers. This spunky woman, who is older than many of the residents, roams the facility's hallways giving hugs, handing out hard candy, and making the residents feel special. "Doing this keeps me young, alive, and sane," she told the reporter.

"I just can't see myself sitting at home in a rocking chair, watching TV, said another volunteer, 87-year-old Judith Chevola. Instead, Chevola and her fellow Golden Gals read to the residents, give them birthday parties, help them with craft projects, and provide the residents with many sympathetic ears.

These 17 women are at a stage in their lives when they could easily fall back on the excuse that they are too old to volunteer. But they know better. Their lives have been enriched, as have the lives of Beth Abraham's residents.

How can you best give the gift of yourself to others? Begin by looking at what you enjoy doing. If you like working with numbers, you could help an elderly or independent mentally handicapped person balance his checkbook. If you sew, a church-sponsored thrift shop could use your skills to repair torn clothing. If you're a gardener, why not lend your talents to beautifying the landscaping at a local community site?

Whatever it is you decide to do, enjoy yourself! And, if possible, draw others in to help you. This shouldn't be difficult. If you're having fun, others will want to join you.

At this point, I want you to think about a way you can give of yourself. Maybe the following statement, filled in by you, will help you focus on a particular action:

By the end of, I will give my talent of _____.

3. Give Financial Support. You've been to church and heard the sermons about tithing. I won't overemphasize the message, because I know you've heard it all before. But, from my own experience, I know that tithing works. When I give, blessings always flow back to me in great abundance.

Giving financial support to worthy organizations may seem difficult, especially if you are just making ends meet, but if you experiment with the concept for one month, you'll see that you'll get back much more than you gave.

Here's what happened to one man who gave.

This man wanted to start a trucking business, so he saved until he had enough to secure a loan. The banker he dealt with ran the necessary checks and considered the man a safe risk. When the time came for the loan to be made, the man borrowing the money asked the banker to put one-tenth of the loan amount into a special account. "That's the Lord's money," he explained. "I thought for sure I was dealing with a crackpot," the banker said.

As weeks passed, the banker watched as the businessman used the "Lord's account" to give money to charity and religious causes. Little by little, the man kept depositing into that special account. After six years of this activity, the banker realized that this man was not crazy, for his business flourished and he kept giving away more and more money. He was doing something right!

Have you been giving financial support to your church and to organizations you believe do good work? Take a look at how much you give. Can you give a little more? Perhaps one percent? If you are not comfortable with this, are there other ways you can help raise money for the organizations you want to help?

Here is a brief story about one man who found a great way to help his church. His story appears in the book, *Turning Needs to Deeds,* published by the editors of *Guideposts.*

Every Tuesday evening, sometimes until three o'clock in the morning, Richard Henry bakes pies.

On Wednesday, Richard sells his pies. By early afternoon, he has sold from 60 to 100 pies, whatever he was able to bake the night before.

Richard Henry has a regular job. He doesn't do this to support himself. He does it to help his church. So far, his pie sales have brought his church anywhere from $1500 to $2000 each year!

Mr. Henry gives. The man with the trucking business gives. The Golden Gals give. All do so in their own way, and they all do it throughout the year. So can you!

All year long, give your faith, your time, and your support in as many ways as possible. Bring the satisfying spirit of giving to your everyday life.

Generous people are rarely mentally ill.

—Dr. Karl Menninger